TH

The Michigan Eco-Traveler

A GUIDE TO SUSTAINABLE ADVENTURES IN THE GREAT LAKES STATE

Sally Barber

The University of Michigan Press
Ann Arbor

This book may not be reproduced, in whole or in part, including illustrations, in any form (beyond that copying permitted by Sections 107 and 108 of the U.S. Copyright Law and except by reviewers for the public press), without written permission from the publisher.

Published in the United States of America by
The University of Michigan Press
Manufactured in the United States of America
⊗ Printed on acid-free paper

2017   2016   2015   2014   4   3   2   1

A CIP catalog record for this book is available from the British Library.

Library of Congress Cataloging-in-Publication Data

Barber, Sally.
    The Michigan eco-traveler : a guide to sustainable adventures in the Great Lakes state / Sally Barber.
        pages   cm
    Includes bibliographical references and index.
    ISBN 978-0-472-03530-4 (pbk. : alk. paper) — ISBN 978-0-472-02916-7 (e-book)
    1. Ecotourism—Michigan—Guidebooks.   2. Michigan—Guidebooks.   I. Title.
    G156.5.E26B35 2014
    917.7404—dc23
    2013036758

To Michigan explorers yet to be born.

May you also find joy in discovering Michigan's natural treasures.

CONTENTS

Introduction

Michigan's natural world is a kaleidoscope of life. Our meadows, wetlands, waters, woods, and farmland provide an ever-changing show. This display once offered the population a sensory-rich, animated backdrop for living out daily lives. The course of time redirected many of us from rural settings to urban centers. The twenty-first century finds nearly 76 percent of midwesterners have adopted city life. We've traded natural landscapes for skyscrapers, strip malls, and a neighborhood park here and there. But as much as we might love the urban lifestyle, no amount of concrete and steel seems to extinguish our instinct to explore, connect with nature, and investigate fresh horizons.

Responding to nature's beckoning helps us regain inner balance and a sense of wonder, while affording us means to test personal limits. Several buzz terms are tossed around these days to describe travel and outdoor recreational experiences. Labels we hear are *ecotourism, nature-based tourism, responsible and sustainable tourism*, and now, *eco-explorer*. What do they mean and where do we fit?

Michigan abounds with nature-based tourism, but nature-based tourism is not always environmentally friendly. For example, ATVs carelessly blazing through natural landscapes can harm ecosystems, although the activity is nature-based. Ecotourism emerged in the 1970s from a blossoming environmental movement. It involves more than eco-friendly recreation. The International Ecotourism Society is a nonprofit organization advocating principles of sustainability. It defines ecotourism as "responsible travel to natural areas that conserves the environment and improves the well-being of local people." It is intimately tied to benefiting local economies. Sustainable tourism is defined by the United Nations World Tourism Organization as "tourism that meets the needs of present tourists and host regions while protecting and enhancing opportunity for the future." Simply put, responsible travel embraces the benefits, and limits damaging aspects of tourism.

The eco-explorer is a new breed. *Eco-explorer* describes the individual who bends to the inner call to travel and recreate without negatively impacting ecosystems—and more. It's the person willing to adopt a thoughtful new ethic—a commitment to minimizing their environmental impact when pursuing outdoor recreation. It is the eco-tourist, the responsible tourist, and the nature explorer all in one curious, adventurous package.

It's hard to imagine a more perfect location for the eco-explorer than Michigan. The state's been dubbed the Great Lakes State, Winter Wonderland, Pure Michigan, and of course, the place to seek a Pleasant Peninsula. Eco-explorers, hold onto your hats. The Mitten has 3,288 miles of Great Lakes coastline, 11,000 inland lakes, 75,000 acres of sand dunes, and 19.3 million acres of forest to explore. Along with it, we have a well-established recreation infrastructure and deeply entrenched outdoor traditions. These assets converge to create the playground of the Midwest and extraordinary opportunities to connect to your inner explorer.

The purpose of this book is to unveil possibilities for enjoying low-impact experiences in the Mitten State. You'll find a sampling of classic Michigan and little-known gems to whet your appetite for sustainable fun. These pages celebrate the fact that being an eco-explorer in no way diminishes opportunities for rewarding outdoor experiences. But being an eco-explorer does ask something of us. It requires raising our awareness and giving careful consideration to our actions. It calls for taking responsibility for the consequences of our recreational activities. It asks that we refuse to exploit the natural world and that we accept and forward new recreational standards.

We choose to adopt a low-impact ethic to preserve nature's treasures because it is in the interest of the earth's long-term health, as well as our own well-being. Modern society demands we spend prolonged periods before electronic screens. Connected has come to mean we are engaged technologically, rather than interacting with the three-dimensional, multisensory world around us. Without realizing it, life has closed in. But nature resurrects dulled spirits. It fully engages our senses to re-awaken us to the powers within. In nature, we hear, see, feel, smell, and touch profound mysteries. We are challenged physically and spiritually by outdoor experiences, whether tackling a mountain on skis, paddling a fast-moving river, or gazing at silver moonlight reflected on still waters. In nature, we discover we are more than we ever thought we were.

This book introduces you to sustainable practices developed and developing across Michigan which support outdoor recreation platforms. You will see how each segment of the recreation industry confronts unique issues in the greening process. New products and equipment enter the marketplace every day helping businesses and organizations convert to more sustainable methods. But there are basic sustainability principles the eco-explorer can apply to judge a venue's progress on the green path. In a nutshell, essential practices address waste management, energy use, water conservation, and reduction in the use of toxic chemicals.

Good reader, beware. Not every activity or facility branded "green" lives up to its promotion. There are businesses out there willing to exaggerate sustainability accomplishments to win patronage. The environmental organization Greenpeace calls the deceptive practice "greenwashing." Greenwashing can take various forms, according to Greenpeace. A company may boast of an environmental achievement when the measure is required by law. A business may tout an environmental accomplishment to distract attention from other ecologically damaging practices. There are endless tricks and it can be quite difficult to sift marketing fiction from fact.

To help you evaluate experiences, each chapter of this book contains an eco-checklist relevant to the type of venue showcased in that chapter. The list aids you in understanding how you can be a responsible explorer and helps you assess what vital steps a business or facility has accomplished. It's up to you to keep your eyes and ears open and ask questions of venues. Keep in mind that some well-intentioned facilities are limited by what products are currently available, or by law. Realize the greening of Michigan's hospitality and recreation industry is an evolution. It's a vital transformation affording each of us the chance to participate.

Partnership is a key component to forwarding the greening of our recreation. Resorts, parks, and hotels collaborate with local, state, and federal government authorities to advance sustainability and build tourism infrastructure. In turn, facilities ask for the cooperation of patrons. Hotels may request patrons forego housekeeping services. Parks may ask visitors to reduce electric usage. Small steps, multiplied by hundreds of eco-explorers, create sustainability.

Each chapter concludes with an in-depth look at a related topic highlighting sustainable contributions of Michigan's pioneering individuals, businesses, and conservationists.

Sustainability Begins at Home

If we are intent on preserving Michigan's natural resources for the next generation to enjoy, there are positive changes every eco-explorer can immediately adopt. Fortunately, reducing the environmental impact of our outdoor experiences is quite doable. We may lessen our footprint by reducing the number of getaways we take, by taking fewer getaways but staying longer, or by exploring close to home. Every county in Michigan offers interesting places to enjoy, trails, waterways, and wildlife. Some of your best opportunities may be just down the road. That's eco-explorer thinking!

In the case of most recreational getaways, transportation is the leading offender in creating a negative eco-footprint and typically the greatest contributor of greenhouse gas emissions. Of all transport means, air travel causes the highest levels of greenhouse gas emissions. In some areas of the state, it may be possible to access the more eco-friendly public rail or bus transportation, but for the most part, Michigan explorers rely on passenger vehicles to get to their favorite recreational haven. If circumstances allow, consider renting or borrowing a hybrid car for your next adventure.

A significant step in greening your experience is to estimate your trip's carbon footprint. Online calculators allow you to determine the carbon footprint for your specific vehicle and the distance you expect to drive. The calculator found at http://calculator.carbonfootprint.com/calculator.aspx allows you to compare the footprint for various modes of transportation for a specific trip. Add estimates for lodging and dining impact for your total.

Once you've calculated your getaway's carbon impact, you might consider offsetting. Carbon offsets allow you to counteract a trip's impact by funding projects that offset greenhouse gas emissions. Replanting rainforests and funding of wind farms are common offsets, but there are several options. TerraPass (www.terrapass.com) allows individuals to purchase carbon offsets in custom amount units of 1,000 pounds. Make offsetting more personal by planting a tree or two in your own yard or community.

Investing a few minutes researching your destination before making your escape paves the way for green fun. More than anything, the new eco-explorer ethic requires greater attention to the consequences of our activities. With the help of this book, you can find the greenest choices in lodging and recreation for your adventure. You might also want to scope out locations for green entertainment venues and farmers markets for obtaining locally produced food.

You're packed and pumped, but before closing the door behind you, green the home front. Conservation tips we've heard hundreds of times are easy to overlook, like properly inflating your vehicle's tires and making sure the vehicle is operating at peak efficiency. Take a moment to dial down the hot-water heater and unplug electronics. These are simple but meaningful measures. If it isn't yet your habit, now is a good time to include it in your routine.

Michigan state parks, just one of the state's outstanding recreation venues, welcome more than 20 million visitors annually, and national parks in Michigan see more than 2 million visitors each year. Overall, more than 74 million leisure travelers enjoy the state in any given year, according to the Michigan Economic Development Corporation. Imagine the positive effect if every traveler and adventurer took small steps to green their getaways. Take the challenge. Lead the way. We each have the power to protect and sustain the Michigan we love to explore.

CHAPTER 1

Sail Away with Me

One need only conjure the image of a tall ship's billowing sails and graceful contour to unleash an inner longing for freedom, romance, and adventure. Powered by wind, Michigan's historic tall ship fleet is the poster child for inspired eco-adventures. A tall ship cruise creates a natural link to nature's sublime trio—water, air, and weather. Help hoist sails in the seafaring tradition, or sit back and take in breathtaking Great Lakes scenery, confident in the knowledge that your freshwater voyage is as environmentally friendly as it is exciting.

Compare the footprint of a tall ship sail with other types of recreational boating. The U.S. Environmental Protection Agency acknowledged that a 70-horsepower, 2-stroke engine (power for a majority of recreational boats) operating for 60 minutes releases as much hydrocarbon pollution as an automobile travelling 5,000 miles. Considered a primary cause of water pollution, the annual volume of hydrocarbon and oil pollution in North American waters from recreational boating is thought to be 15 times more than the amount of the Exxon Valdez spill. Now, rethink the eco value of a wind-powered cruise.

The Mitten State is fortunate to host four tall ship companies, each offering an exhilarating itinerary of Great Lakes sails. From regular two-hour sails to multiday voyages, to charters, specialty, and educational sails, you can tailor a trip to your own sea adventure vision. Visit charming and historical ports. Explore uninhabited islands. Discover Great Lakes marine life while taking part in seafaring traditions. The tall ship experience is an awakening to just how fun a green adventure can be. If you catch the sailing bug, you might consider a high-action experience like kiteboarding, or curing cabin fever with an ice-sailing experience.

Cruising Lake Huron

BaySail
107 5th Street
Bay City, Michigan 48708
(989) 895-5193
www.baysailbaycity.org
Vessels: *Appledore IV, Appledore V*

BaySail is a private, nonprofit organization focused on promoting environmental stewardship of Lake Huron's Saginaw Bay and the Great Lakes. Each year, between 8,000 and 9,000 individuals enjoy sails aboard BaySail's schooners, the *Appledore IV* and the *Appledore V.* From April through October, opportunities exist for public sails, overnight voyaging for adults and youth, school groups, and charters. Specialty programs range from dinner sails to stargazing sails to the popular "Legends of the Saginaw Sail." The Legends sail takes passengers cruising along the riverfront into Saginaw Bay. River history is presented by a historian with live maritime music adding authenticity to the experience. Fall-color tours provide a venue for taking in the region's spectacular autumn show. Every year, BaySail is involved in port visits to a changing lineup of locations including Detroit; Cleveland, Ohio; Erie,

Fig. 1. The historic replica *Friends Good Will* tall ship sets sail from her South Haven home port for a Pirate Chasers Adventure Sail. The specialty sail allows children to play buccaneer and capture seafaring scoundrels. Credit: Michigan Maritime Museum.

Pennsylvania; Green Bay, Wisconsin; the Gulf of Mexico; the Atlantic Coast; Nova Scotia; and other locales.

With skilled captains at the helm, the *Appledore IV* and the *Appledore V* ply nimbly across the waters, their sails cracking in response to cool lake breezes. Both are two-masted schooners, reminiscent of the vessels which sailed the lakes during the early years of the Great Lakes shipping industry. The schooners are licensed by the U.S. Coast Guard and meet all safety regulations.

The 85-foot *Appledore IV* was built in 1989. It's licensed to carry 52 passengers and sleeps 14. More than 3,500 square feet of sails catch the wind to power this handsome vessel. The ship sails from Water Street docks in downtown Bay City, a historic maritime district. The 65-foot *Appledore V* was built in 1992. This snowbird schooner is based in Key West, Florida, in the winter and Bay City during the summer months. It's licensed to carry 32 passengers and sleeps 12.

BaySail's educational programming is nationally recognized. Its EcoSail youth program focuses on traditional Great Lakes maritime traditions and sailing techniques and also offers hands-on study of the ecosystem. The organization is involved in raising funds to construct a 6,000-square foot environmental education center along the Saginaw River. The planned green public education center will be the first of its kind amidst the Great Lakes.

BaySail's Great Lakes stewardship mission prompts a variety of measures to create the most eco-friendly sailing experience possible. When winds fail to meet power needs, ship auxiliary engines are engaged. The *Appledore V* has a 90-horsepower engine. The *Appledore IV* has a 135-horsepower engine. Both engines are powered by marine diesel fuel consisting of 10 percent biofuel. A scheduled sail is typically powered 50 percent by the engine and 50 percent by Mother Nature. The engine also charges batteries for ship lighting.

Due to logistical issues, a program to serve locally produced foods to passengers is not in place. Instead, food service is catered. However, BaySail encourages caterers to use environmentally friendly disposable plates and utensils and initiated a switch from boxed meals to a greener bag presentation. A diesel marine stove is used to cook onboard, when needed. The company adheres to a policy prohibiting the purchase of bottled water. Instead, a cooler and paper cups are used to quench passengers' thirst.

As required of all Great Lakes ships, a holding tank is employed for human waste, which is pumped out to a local land sewer system for disposal. Other types of waste are sorted and properly disposed, with recyclables taken to a recycling center. Waste oil is also recycled.

Voyagers bring their own bedding for overnights on the *Appledore* ships, eliminating the need for BaySail to launder linens. Thus, passengers are personally responsible for pursuing nontoxic laundering methods.

BaySail and other tall ship operators have a common conundrum. Eco-friendly marine maintenance products have been slow in hitting the market. Bottom paints traditionally contained high concentrations of heavy metals, which are harmful to the ecosystem, but BaySail uses a newer, eco-friendly bottom paint. As of publication, eco-friendly oils and lubricants necessary for onboard maintenance remain difficult to obtain.

BaySail, the Inland Seas Association, Michigan State University's Sea Grant Extension Program, and Grand Valley State University Annis Water Resource Institute partnered in a federally funded program in 2011 and 2012 called Making the Great Lakes Great. The educational program involved public workshops, dockside tours, and cruises on Lakes Michigan, Huron, and Erie.

The *Appledore IV* and *V* are good choices to enjoy experiencing Great Lakes ports and educational sails.

Set Sail on Lake Michigan

Michigan Maritime Museum
260 Dyckman Avenue
South Haven, Michigan 49090
(269) 637-8078
www.michiganmaritimemuseum.org
Vessel: *Friends Good Will*

The Michigan Maritime Museum in South Haven operates the sloop *Friends Good Will*. The ship is a replica of a merchant vessel built in 1810.

Involved in the War of 1812, the original ship has a storied history. Sailing Lake Michigan, the museum's *Friends Good Will* is a 101-square-foot topsail vessel with a passenger capacity of 28. It's a member of Tall Ships America, a nonprofit organization dedicated to preserving the tall ship culture. The ship is the only tall ship on the Great Lakes featuring an interactive, state-of-the-art classroom for year-round instruction.

Friends Good Will is fully U.S. Coast Guard approved for passengers. Operators offer three daily passenger sails during peak season. It also provides educational sails and charters. Among its most unique offerings is the 90-minute Pirate Chaser Sail. The ship's six-pound pivot canon adds authenticity to the adventure. Geared for youngsters and families, passengers role-play, capturing scoundrels and sharing in their loot.

Friends Good Will uses a 170-horsepower diesel engine in leaving and entering the docks. More than two-thirds of every sail is wind-powered. A battery system provides any needed electricity. Onboard food service is limited, but the ship features a traditional wood cook stove with propane backup.

The Michigan Maritime Museum also offers a six-mile cruise along the Black River in the electric launch *Lindy Lou*. The vessel is a replica of launches used in West Michigan between the 1890s and 1930s to transport tourists to resorts. The *Lindy Lou* provides all the advantages of electric power advocated by environmentalists.

The *Friends Good Will* and the *Lindy Lou* are nice choices for young families and for those who would enjoy learning more about Great Lakes history and culture at the maritime museum.

Traverse Tall Ships Co.
13240 S. West Bay Shore Drive
Traverse City, Michigan 49684
(231) 941-2000
www.tallshipsailing.com
Vessel: *Manitou*

In 2012, the Traverse Tall Ship Company marked its twenty-fifth season of cruising the beautiful Grand Traverse Bay. The company operates the 59-passenger *Manitou*, a replica of a 1800s "coasting" cargo schooner. Built in 1983, the 114-foot ship sails out of Traverse City between Memorial Day and early October. As many as 10,000 passengers enjoy sails onboard the *Manitou* each year. The ship meets or exceeds all U.S. Coast Guard regulations. Adventuring opportunities abound with three daily sails, specialty cruises, multiday sails, and the *Manitou's* onboard bed and breakfast. Autumn multiday sails showcase the fall color palette and explore Grand Traverse Bay's islands; Beaver Island; also, Cathead Bay along the Leelanau Peninsula; and Old Mission Harbor.

The *Manitou's* auxiliary engine is a 150-horsepower diesel model. About one gallon of fuel is consumed on each regular voyage as the vessel's engine pulls the ship out to open water and returns it to its dock. Over the course of a season, only 300 gallons of diesel fuel is typically consumed.

A traditional marine wood cook stove is the galley centerpiece. Every effort is made to incorporate local foods into the ship's meal service. Cooks garner ingredients from the local farmers market to keep the menu fresh. Regular afternoon sails feature locally made Moomers Ice Cream, named the number one ice cream in the nation by ABC's *Good Morning America*. Wine- and microbrew-tasting sails also feature local products. Food is served on biodegradable disposable plates, while recyclable plastic cups are used to serve beverages. All recyclable bottles, cans, cups, and other items are sent to American Waste & Recycling, northern Michigan's only locally owned and operated garbage collection and recycling center. Guest bedding is laundered by a linen service using unknown products. As with the other tall ship companies, finding eco-friendly ship maintenance and cleaning products is a challenge, but every attempt is made to avoid runoff into the eco-system.

The *Manitou* is a good choice for specialty cruises, multiday sails, and as a day trip incorporated into a Traverse City area vacation.

Superior Voyages

Superior Odyssey
P.O. Box 672
Marquette, Michigan 49855
Docked at Marquette's Lower Harbor

(906) 361-3668
www.superiorodyssey.com
Vessel: *Odyssey II*

Superior Odyssey is a family operation that launched in 2009. The 58-foot schooner *Odyssey II* is owned by Niko and Jill Economides. The vessel sails from Marquette to Lake Superior destinations between mid-May and mid-October. Unlike tall ships operated by other Michigan companies, the *Odyssey II* is a National Registered Historic Coaster Schooner built in 1933. She sailed both the Atlantic and Pacific before coming to the Great Lakes. The *Odyssey II* features a wooden hull. She is gaff-rigged with top sails and is an example of the workhorse ship of the golden age of commercial sailing. The ship is licensed by the U.S. Coast Guard.

The *Odyssey II* carries up to six passengers for a more interactive sailing experience. The company offers regular two-hour sails. Also available are four-hour sails to Presque Isle, White Rocks, and Middle Isle Bay. Eight-hour voyages to Presque Isle offer opportunities to explore remote Lake Superior islands. Overnight voyages to Huron Islands or Pictured Rocks National Lakeshore at Munising provide a lengthier taste of the seafaring experience. Fewer recreational boats populate Lake Superior than Lakes Huron and Michigan, making the *Odyssey II* voyages a quiet, intimate encounter with nature.

The *Odyssey II* passengers take personal responsibility for making their voyage sustainable. Food service is typically unavailable onboard; however, the ship has a traditional wood-burning cook stove for use as needed. The ship owners also operate an orchard and maple syrup operation and feature their harvest when possible. When food is provided, an effort is made to work with the Marquette food co-op to incorporate local products. Most passengers bring food onboard and take their trash with them. Any trash left onboard is recycled. Overnight passengers bring their own bedding.

The *Odyssey II*'s auxiliary engine is a 65-horsepower diesel model. Typically, the engine is engaged only when moving through the inner harbor. When possible, the captain sails up to the dock. The smallest of the Great Lakes tall ship fleet, over the course of a season the *Odyssey II* consumes only 10 gallons of diesel fuel.

Awareness of the negative environmental impact of many ship main-tenance products prompts the company's limited use of harmful prod-ucts, especially bottom paints.

The *Odyssey II* is a good choice for those wishing to exercise control over their eco-footprint, for sailing to remote destinations, and for an affordable lakes adventure.

Extreme Sailing

ICE BOATING

A simple sail, sled, and wings create one of Michigan's most exciting sus-tainable winter sports, ice sailing. Frigid temperatures and speeds up to 100 miles per hour form a cloud of danger, making the lake sport ideal for extreme adventurers. Ice sailing, also known as ice boating and ice yachting, is an activity dating back to northern Europe's Viking days. It came to Michigan in the mid-1930s. Today, the state is one of the most popular ice-sailing destinations in the nation.

Ice boats are typically designed to carry a single individual across frozen lakes or fields. Sailing an ice craft requires skills similar to water sailing, but its capacity for high speeds demands greater control over the craft.

Although the sport is highly weather dependent, the ice-sailing sea-son usually begins after the Christmas holiday, when lakes are frozen to a depth of at least five inches. Several cities serve as sweet spots for ice-boat enthusiasts and competition hosts. St. Ignace is home to the World Ice and Snow Championships, but racing takes place across the state. Clubs exist in Kalamazoo, Muskegon, Bay City, Traverse City, Elk Rap-ids, and southeast Michigan. The lovely sight of full sails gliding across a frozen lake draws spectators, as well as sailors, to this timeless pursuit.

KITEBOARDING

In 2008, the International Sailing Association approved kiteboarding as an international sailing class. The extreme surface water sport gained a following in the 1990s that increases each year. Participants can be seen sailing across waters and waves all along Michigan's coastline. The gear required for kiteboarding is simple. All that is needed is a board, harness, control bar, and a large kite. Kites come in various sizes and shapes rated for wind speeds and boarder skill level. Freestyle kiteboarders incorporate jumps and moves into their ride. The fun isn't limited to water. Equipment can be adapted for kiteboarding on grass, sand, and snow.

While the wind-powered sport is free from the use of fossil fuels, equipment and gear is another story. However, the availability of bamboo boards and petroleum-free board waxes is increasing.

Favorite Michigan kiteboarding destinations include Tawas Point, Lexington, Port Huron, Metro Beach, Muskegon, St. Joseph, Saugatuck, and Grand Haven.

Eco Checklist for Extreme and Group Sailing

Is your personal equipment and gear eco-friendly?
What is a ship's auxiliary power source? How often is the engine engaged?
Does food service include locally produced items?
What is the onboard cooking power source?
Are disposable or biodegradable plates, utensils, and packaging used in food service?
How is waste handled?
What general recycling practices are employed?
If cabin bedding is provided, is it laundered with bio-friendly products?
What eco-friendly products are used in ship maintenance?

Explore the Depths of Thunder Bay

There's no better place to dive into Great Lakes maritime history than the remarkable Thunder Bay—an underwater museum where exploration and discovery continue to regularly occur. Thunder Bay chronicles the intriguing and dangerous tale of commercial shipping along the sweetwater seas.

When the first major European ship to sail the Great Lakes went missing on its maiden voyage in the late seventeenth century, it served as clear warning to the danger lurking within the vast waters. It was Rene-Robert de La Salle, an early French explorer of the Great Lakes region, who sailed the first ship. The *Griffon* made its way from Niagara to Green Bay, Wisconsin, in late summer 1679. She disappeared on her return to Niagara that fall and was never heard from again. La Salle's vessel became the first Great Lakes ghost ship.

So treacherous are the Great Lakes waters, it is estimated more than 6,000 ships have succumbed to its forces—majestic schooners similar to the *Manitou* and the *Friends Good Will*, steamers, and even modern freighters. The watery grave of these many ships forms one of Michigan's most significant historical sites, Thunder Bay National Marine Sanctuary and Underwater Preserve. The sanctuary is situated along the bottomland of northwest Lake Huron in what was dubbed by early sailors as "Shipwreck Alley." In and near the sanctuary's 448 square miles, more than 200 ships met their demise during the last two centuries, their fatal destiny frozen in time by the cold Lake Huron waters of Thunder Bay.

Thunder Bay was declared Michigan's first Great Lakes Bottomland Preserve in 1981. In 2000, it was designated Thunder Bay National Marine Sanctuary and Underwater Preserve, bearing the distinction of being the first freshwater and Great Lakes sanctuary, and the first to concentrate exclusively on an underwater collection of cultural resources. Its mission is to protect the cultural treasure, improve scientific knowledge of the resource, and further understanding of maritime heritage.

The shipwreck collection, docks, and piers under the sanctuary's protection span the history of Great Lakes shipping industry and ship architecture. Many of the nearly 100 discovered wrecks remain amazingly intact. Unlike ocean wrecks, the cold freshwater minimizes deterioration of sunken vessels, cargo, and the personal items of crew members. Sadly, the integrity of these valuable, living history lessons is threatened today by nonnative zebra mussel colonies encrusting wrecks. With no solution in sight, historic wrecks face a second disaster from the nuisance mollusk.

The one-of-a-kind shipwreck collection makes Thunder Bay a popular dive site. But nondivers find that several wrecks are viewable from the surface. Rentals are available for clear-bottomed kayaks and glass-bottom boat tours are offered.

Unique learning opportunities are found at the Great Lakes Maritime Heritage Center, located in Alpena along the shores of Thunder Bay. The center provides 9,000 square feet of exhibit area showcasing Great Lakes artifacts. The centerpiece of the free facility is a life-size replica schooner complete with visual and sound effects re-creating the experience of sailing through a Great Lakes storm. The Thunder Bay Sanctuary Resource Collection, housed at the George N. Fletcher Public Library in Alpena, contains 65,000 photos, as well as charts, periodicals, and files pertaining to 20,000 Great Lakes vessels. It's an eco-explorer's paradise.

Great Lakes Maritime Heritage Center
500 West Fletcher Street
Alpena, Michigan 49707
(989) 356-8805
www.thunderbay.noaa.gov

CHAPTER 2

Sustainable Slopes

When the flurries fly, Michigan snowbirds scatter to warm climates, while the more hardy among us belt out refrains of "Let it Snow." Skiers and boarders dust off their equipment as they wait for the magic moment when resorts announce opening day. It's a Mitten State tradition generations in the making.

Michigan is a proud contributor to the growth of slope sports. The U.S. Ski and Snowboard Association, the governing body for Olympic skiing and snowboarding, originated in the Upper Peninsula community of Ishpeming in 1905. Home to the U.S. National Ski Hall of Fame, the city is considered the nation's birthplace of organized skiing. Snowboarding, too, had its start in Michigan. In 1965, Muskegonite Sherman Poppen devised the forerunner of the modern snowboard for his children. His invention earned Poppen the title Father of Snowboarding.

The state's enthusiasm for winter slope sports is undeniable. With 51 ski areas, Michigan has more places to downhill ski and snowboard than any other state in the country except New York. More than 250 chairlifts, 1,000 runs, and 50 terrain parks offer a range of opportunities to experience the intoxicating thrill of going one-on-one with a mountain. But the exhilarating sport is not without environmental costs.

The practice of snowmaking is one of the industry's greatest conundrums. The downhill-ski industry's big ticket is a pristine natural environment clothed in fresh powder. But the process of keeping slopes white can threaten local ecosystems, especially when under pressures from climate change—a new twist to the slope problem. "Economic Impact of Climate Change in Michigan," an assessment by the University of Maryland, reports climate change will decrease the ski season in the

Fig. 2. Snow guns blanket slopes at Crystal Mountain Resort in Thompsonville. The resort's new high-efficiency pipeline supplies water to the snowmaking system. Credit: Crystal Mountain Resort & Spa.

state by as much as 65 percent by 2050. According to the study, warmer temperatures and increased winter rainfalls will force ski areas to increase reliance on artificial snow in order to remain economically viable. Drought in the age of climate change may compound problems. Lack of natural snow and rain reduces water levels in streams, rivers, lakes, and aquifers needed to produce snow.

The environmental footprint for snowmaking is high. Snow machines add visual and noise pollution and consume huge amounts of water and energy. Even the most energy-efficient snowmaking system can account for up to 67 percent of a ski area's energy consumption, according to the trade publication *Ski Area Management*.

Ski area water systems built to support snowmaking can be as large as that of small communities. While snow-machine efficiency continues to improve and varies among resort systems, to cover one acre in a foot of snow requires about 140,000 gallons of water. Harbor Springs' Nub's Nob reports on its website that its system feeds 282 patented snow guns covering 97 percent of the ski area's 248 acres of skiable terrain. The system uses five high-pressure pumps to supply water to over 23 miles of underground pipe at 46 slopes. At full capacity, a total of 5,000 gallons of water per minute is used at Nub's to create snow. Even the best snow-makers are energy eaters. In the case of Nub's Nob, the snowmaking fleet's electric motors use 5,200 horsepower when operating at capacity.

Mother Nature knows how to balance the resource, but do we? Over-use of the water resource at ski areas can threaten aquatic life, wetlands, and water flow and tables. Environmentalists concerned about snow-making suggest the slower melt rate of denser machine-made snow negatively impacts vegetation growth and influences melt rate of natu-ral snow. This raises concern regarding the impact on the availability of spring vegetation for forage, which is critical to wildlife. Chemical and biological additives commonly used to enhance snowmaking efficiency may pose long-term issues for the ecosystem, although long-term im-pact studies are still needed.

A downhill area's energy use and carbon footprint stems not only from snowmaking, but also from chairlifts. Energy-guzzling lifts are ex-pensive to replace with higher-efficiency models, and so the conversion to high-performance lifts takes place over time. Slope energy revolu-tions are unlikely to happen. At least one resort took steps to counteract the chairlift issue. Benzie County's Crystal Mountain Resort and Spa requires 125,000 kilowatts annually to power its high-speed chairlift. (An average home uses 9,000 kilowatts per year.) Since 2007 the resort has purchased wind-energy credits for its lift. In a single season, the measure prevents adding 174,000 pounds of carbon dioxide to the envi-ronment, the equivalent of driving a car eight times around the planet.

Another primary consideration for the responsible skier and board-er, is a resort's land use practices and development. Unless ecosystem preservation is a focus, construction of new trails, lodging expansions, and other facilities may increase stress and damage on valuable natural areas.

It's easy to see that keeping slope sports fun while preserving the mountain's integrity and ensuring profitability is a tightrope walk for resort operators. In 2000, the National Ski Areas Association (NSAA) adopted a Sustainable Slopes Initiative to help ski-area owners and operators raise the bar on industry environmental standards. The initiative establishes voluntary best practices for resorts across the country. The charter's 21 principles address water and energy use, forest management, air quality, and recycling. By 2012, four Michigan ski areas had endorsed the charter, including Crystal Mountain, Nub's Nob, The Homestead in Glen Arbor, and Mount Bohemia—located in the Upper Peninsula's Keweenaw Peninsula. The measure brings slope preservation into the spotlight; however, some environmentalists complain the voluntary charter is ineffective and does little to protect natural assets. Others criticize the effort as industry greenwashing.

Environmental ethics and practices will continue to evolve through stakeholder commitment, as well as science and technology advancements. Whether you're a novice on the slopes or an expert, if you choose an eco-friendly ski area for your next downhill adventure, you'll cast a vote to preserve the experience for the long term. Before leaving home, check a ski area's website to learn about its sustainable practices and select your facility thoughtfully. You can also do your part by buying environmentally friendly ski and snowboard wax to avoid leaving chemical residue on the slopes as with traditional waxes. If possible, purchase green equipment, such as bamboo skis and organic clothing. Your efforts make a difference. The longevity of downhill sports is on the line.

Downhill Areas

Boyne Resorts
www.boyne.com

Boyne Highlands
600 Highland Drive
Harbor Springs, Michigan 49740
(231) 526-3000

Boyne Mountain
1 Boyne Mountain Road
Boyne Falls, Michigan 49713
(231) 549-6000

Boyne Highlands and Boyne Mountain, the two largest ski resorts in Michigan, have taken some giant steps in sustainability. Boyne is the first resort operation to offset its carbon footprint through partnership with Cool Earth, an international organization dedicated to protecting ecosystems and combatting global warming. For each ton of carbon dioxide generated by Boyne lifts, lodges, and vehicles, two tons of equivalent emissions are prevented through the company's investment in the Cool Earth rainforest protection program. Over a one-year period, Boyne covers twice its carbon emissions.

Boyne Mountain in Boyne Falls and nearby Boyne Highlands in Harbor Springs together offer over 850 skiable acres. A variety of options make Boyne family friendly for winter recreation. The two locations feature 115 downhill runs, several terrain parks, and 70 km of cross-country trails. Boyne claims its snow-gun system is the most efficient in the Midwest. The snowmaking operation includes 117 Boyne Low-E fan guns. The Boyne Highlands fleet includes 113 of the same. Boyne's proprietary machines operate 40 percent more efficiently than standard snowmakers, according to the company.

Boyne demonstrates commitment to sustainability across operations. Both locations earned Green Lodging Michigan certifications for implementing eco-friendly practices. In 2010, Boyne Mountain was recognized as the Recycler of the Year by the Charlevoix County Recycling Program.

If downhill sports are not your cup of tea, Boyne ignites wintertime fun with a variety of low-impact activities, including ice skating, dog sledding, tubing, a zip line, and horse-drawn wagon rides.

Crystal Mountain
12500 Crystal Mountain Drive
Thompsonville, Michigan 49683
(231) 378-2000
www.crystalmountain.com

Crystal Mountain is widely recognized for environmental stewardship by groups such as the Michigan Chapter of the Sierra Club. Its eco-friendly practices span the operation without sacrificing the quality experience that led to its ranking among *Condé Nast Traveler*'s 50 best places to ski and stay in North America. The resort offers 45 downhill slopes, 40 km of cross-country trails, and over 80 acres for snowshoe treks. Crystal was the first Michigan ski area and resort to purchase wind-energy credits for powering a chairlift. It continues to add efficient snow guns to its fleet and uses retention ponds for snowmelt, redirecting the water into its golf course. Crystal practices wildlife management through the Wings of Wonder program, a nonprofit rapture sanctuary and rehabilitation facility. It's a member of the Great Lakes Renewable Energy Association and provides an electric vehicle charging station for guests. A free bus service is provided, reducing traffic and pollution. Crystal was also the first four-season resort in the state to earn the highest level of Green Lodging Michigan certification. Green practices are adopted in large and small areas of operation. All new construction is built according to sustainable methods. On a smaller, but notable scale, beverages are served in biodegradable cups and the use of disposable dinnerware has been abandoned. A host of additional measures serve to enhance Crystal's leadership role in greening the resort industry.

Mount Bohemia
Lac La Belle Road
Lac La Belle, Michigan 49950
(231) 420-5405
www.mtbohemia.com

Mount Bohemia marries extreme skiing and sustainability. Situated at the tip of the Keweenaw Peninsula, 15 miles from Copper Harbor, the downhill recreational facility offers backcountry skiing amidst some of the state's most rugged landscape. It features the longest runs with the highest vertical and deepest powder in the Midwest. Seventy-five percent of its 85 trails are gladed runs, the creation of which resulted in minimum disturbance to nature. With annual snowfall totals of 270 inches, the natural winter blanket matches that of Aspen, Colorado. This bountiful gift of snow means Mount Bohemia avoids environmental issues related to snowmaking. The presence of only two lifts also minimizes ecological costs.

Mount Bohemia delivers downhill adventure with a 900-foot vertical drop, cliffs and rocks, twists and turns. The features combine to offer thrilling and challenging runs. But Mount Bohemia fun is not for newbies. Only experienced skiers and riders are permitted here.

Overnighters find simplicity rules in lodging. Yurts provide inexpensive trailside sheltering, enhancing Mount Bohemia's flair for fusing the wilds with the downhill experience.

Missaukee Mountain
6500 West Walker Road
Lake City, Michigan 49651
(231) 839-7575 or (231) 839-4969
http://www.lakecitymich.com/missaukee-ski-mountain.html

Missaukee Mountain is compact, family friendly, and completely in harmony with the whims of nature. The facility is one of a handful of Michigan's remaining community-operated ski areas. Located just outside Lake City, the ski area demonstrates the concept "less is more" when it comes to slope sustainability. A nonprofit facility, Missaukee Mountain spans only 15 acres. It is without snowmaking or night-lighting and is only open weekends and during school Christmas break. The trip to the top of the mountain is via traditional tow ropes operated by volunteers.

Opened in the 1950s, Missaukee Mountain is no slacker when it comes to the downhill experience. With a 500-foot vertical drop, the two moderate runs and one difficult run offer skiers and boarders a rewarding ride. The bunny hill provides a relaxed environment for novices to learn and practice skills. The ski area also offers five miles of trails for Nordic skiers and snowshoe enthusiasts. Everyone is invited to bring their own tubes and sleds to enjoy the free sledding hill. Rentals, hot chocolate, and snacks are available at the lodge.

Eco Checklist for Downhill Areas

Does the ski area have an environmental management plan?
What are the resort's snowmaking water use practices?

How energy efficient is the snowmaking equipment?
Are additives used in snowmaking? If so, what types?
How energy efficient are resort lifts?
Has the ski area adopted renewable energy?
How are wetlands, vegetation, and riparian areas managed?
Is the area managed in accordance to sustainable practices during
the off-season?
Have lodging, dining, and other resort facilities adopted green
practices?
Does the ski area practice innovation in sustainability?

Twenty-First-Century Snow

When Mother Nature fails to deliver snow, ski areas turn to technology to cover the runs. The genius behind many of the machines dotting Michigan slopes comes from the Midland-based SMI Snow Makers. Since Jim VanderKelen brought the company to Midland in the 1970s, SMI has sold more than 25,000 snowmaking products to more than 800 resorts around the globe. Its machines blanket slopes in China, Switzerland, New Zealand, Finland, and other countries. SMI's high-profile clients include the Russian resort Rosa Khutor, host of the 2014 Winter Olympic Games alpine events.

SMI invests $1 million and thousands of hours annually in researching and developing advancements in snowmaking equipment and systems. The company maintains a 10-million-gallon lake and four pumping stations for product testing. From this state-of-the-art facility, the next generation of more eco-friendly snowmakers may emerge. Fortunately for the cause of sustainability, the company has a track record for pioneering and improving snowmaker efficiency, as well as incorporating sustainability concepts into system designs.

Since 2007, SMI technology tripled the efficiency of its machines in operations above 25 degrees. The colder the temperature the easier it is to make snow, so the capacity to produce a desirable snow base at higher temperatures helps stabilize slope conditions throughout the season. SMI's newest designs crossed the temperature threshold and better convert water to snow, conserving water and energy. SMI systems incorporate large reservoirs and maximize the benefits of gravity. Roughly 85 percent of the water tapped for its snowmakers returns to the watershed.

The company went high tech in the 2000s. While SMI's snow proprietary software won't replace Mother Nature's touch, it takes a stab at it with a line of sophisticated automated snowmakers. Its Smart-Snow™ software, combined with high-performance machinery, accurate weather-measuring devices, and auxiliary equipment, produces more snow in less time. SMI efforts to improve efficiency align with the National Ski Areas Association's environmental charter recommendations. The stewardship charter urges ski areas to employ high-performance snowmaking machines in order to minimize negative ecological impact.

SMI stands apart in the world of machine-made snow. It's the only facility on earth integrating research, testing, and production at a single location. Parts are built in-house for the purpose of quality control—and it's right here in Michigan.

Since the 1980s, SMI allowed for retrofitting of older models, a measure supporting sustainable manufacturing programs. Extending the life of snowmaking machines in this way not only benefits the environment—it's a money saver for resorts. New snowmaker models range in price from $2,000 to $30,000, depending on the unit. Operating a fleet of snowmakers can cost a resort millions of dollars each season. The more efficient the snowmaking equipment, the better for the resort, its guests, and the slope's fragile ecosystem.

CHAPTER 3

Paddle Power

The numbers are breathtaking. The reality is thrilling. Michigan has 36,000 miles of rivers and streams, 1,305 square miles of inland water, and 3,288 miles of Great Lakes shoreline. It's no wonder canoeing and kayaking are Mitten State traditions. This vast waterscape, unmatched anywhere in the world, provides a wealth of choices for novice and experienced waterway explorers. A Michigan paddling experience can be as tame as an hour's ride along a gentle river, or as challenging as a multiday, open-water adventure on an unpredictable inland sea.

By nature, the human-powered paddling sport is eco-friendly. But in Michigan, where one is never farther than six miles from a body of water, a resident paddler can launch into a local waterway practically whenever the whim strikes. In launching near home, the paddler minimizes travel, thereby reducing the carbon footprint created by motor-vehicle transportation. According to the University of Michigan's Center for Sustainable Systems, the average car emits 0.86 pounds of carbon dioxide per mile driven, or 43 pounds for a 50-mile trip. Paddling on home waters is truly sustainable fun. It prevents pollution and offers a bonus—the opportunity for an intimate encounter with the natural world of your own home turf.

Extensive marked waterway-destination routes are located across the state, thanks to a grassroots initiative. Ten years ago, a pilot program added new possibilities for low-impact paddling adventures. Michigan Public Act 454 of 2002 involved the Great Lakes Center for Maritime Studies at Western Michigan University; the Michigan Department of

Fig. 3. Kayaks are readied for paddling adventures at William G. Milliken State Park in Detroit, the first urban state park in Michigan. Park lowlands demonstrate the value of wetlands in filtering storm water. Credit: Anita Twardesky, Riverside Kayak Connection.

History, Arts and Libraries; and the Michigan 4-H Youth Conservation Council. The collaborative created the Michigan Heritage Water Trail Program. Program advocates rallied local community support and resources for identifying and developing recreational water pathways. Heritage Water Trails celebrate Michigan's ecological, cultural, economic, educational, and historic legacies. The evolving trail systems showcase significant habitats and geological features and raise awareness of the fragility of waterways to encourage responsible use.

The eight Michigan Heritage Water Trails vary in length, character, required paddling skill, and marked sites. Yet, all reflect the spirit of ecotourism. Each provides interpretive signage along the route highlighting notable historic and natural points. Because many Michigan towns were established along waterways, Heritage Water Trail routes intersect with a variety of communities. Paddlers can count on these large and small communities to welcome the eco-explorer with open arms. Amenities range from shuttle services to campgrounds and picnic areas to restaurants, shops, and hotels.

With so much water comes the burden of responsibility to protect the integrity of Michigan's resource. This is the shared mission of the many volunteers who dedicate time to developing and maintaining heritage blueways. None of the Heritage Water Trails would exist without local recognition of the economic and ecological importance of Michigan's river systems. Each trail is the result of community effort to both preserve and balance environmental and commercial function. Thanks to these hardworking groups, adventurers are afforded the opportunity to explore hundreds of miles of beautiful blueways.

Whether an urbanite or country bumpkin, whether adventuring beneath the silver moon or bright sun, on a still lake, or facing the mighty force of one of the Great Lakes, each dip of the paddle brings the canoer and kayaker closer to Mother Nature's secrets.

Visit the individual Heritage Water Trail websites for additional information and maps to chart a custom paddling excursion.

Custom paddling is also the forte of a growing number of Michigan stand-up paddleboarders (SUP). One of the hottest trends in the paddling world, SUP is practiced on waterways throughout the state.

While catching a wave requires minimal paddling, Great Lakes surfing represents yet another exciting low-impact way to enjoy Michigan's vast water resource.

Michigan Heritage Water Trails

Bangor/South Haven Heritage Water Trail
Van Buren County
H2O_trail@yahoo.com
www.vbco.org/watertrail

The gently flowing Black River is named for its deep, dark color. While rather ominous sounding, the river is actually shallow and friendly, weaving across southwest Michigan's Van Buren and Allegan Counties. The mild current allows paddlers to easily travel up and downstream. A trip along this blueway provides ample opportunity for wildlife sightings. In 2009, the Michigan Department of Environmental Quality documented the Black River Watershed's support of 471 species of plants, 130 species of birds, 70 species of fish, and 67 other species of wildlife.

The Black River played an important role in West Michigan's early development. Industry settled along the river in the mid-1800s, leaving an unfortunate environmental mark. First came the mills, and later a furnace and chemical company. When these industries declined, they left behind a naked landscape. The resilient people of the region found the land suitable for developing a thriving agriculture industry. Along the water trail, 17 marked historic and natural features commemorate the past presence of Native Americans and the area's commercial history.

The Bangor/South Haven Heritage Water Trail is a beauty in all four seasons. The blueway traverses the south branch of the Black River between Bangor and the popular resort town of South Haven. When completed, it will stretch 21 miles to Lake Michigan. A three-mile open section begins at Lion's Park in Bangor and continues to Robert & Merion Horton Memorial Access Site on County Road 687. This section requires about two hours to complete. Eight miles are maintained between the Basic Family Access on County Road 384 and South Haven Black River Park Access on Dunkley Avenue. It's a four-hour paddle to the shining shores of Lake Michigan at South Haven.

The trail is suitable for beginners; however, heavy rains may cause swift currents. Winter paddlers in search of the river's stunning frozen scenery should prepare for harsh conditions.

Detroit Heritage River Water Trail
Detroit, Huron, Rouge and Raisin Rivers
(313) 961–2270
www.michiganwatertrails.org

The Detroit Heritage River Water Trail project encompasses 120 blueway miles stretching from Lake St. Clair to Lake Erie. It features 32 miles along the Detroit River and routes along the Huron, Rouge, and Raisin Rivers. Put in and take out is possible at more than 50 locations. (An adaptive kayak launch is located in Wyandotte.) The trail connects multiple parks, communities, and recreation areas with a wealth of amenities.

This is urban kayaking at its best. Paddle the Detroit River to glide by skyscrapers, freighters, and important landmarks of the War of 1812, the industrial revolution, the Underground Railroad, Prohibition, and more. The route traverses significant natural areas such as the Detroit International Wildlife Refuge, a 5,000 acre habitat for migratory birds. Along the Rouge River in Wyandotte, paddlers pass the site where the famed ship the *Edmund Fitzgerald* was built. Segments circumvent Belle Isle, one of the largest urban parks in the United States, the Lake Erie Metroparks Canals, the Grassy Island Loop adjacent to the shipping channel, and more.

Some paddling experience is required to safely navigate open-water and shipping-channel routes. The paddle from Swan Creek to Lake Erie is an easy loop, providing opportunities to view herons, kingfishers, terns, and the American lotus. The combination of metro sights and nature sanctuaries makes the trail a compelling water adventure.

Drummond Island Heritage Water Trail
Chippewa County
(906) 493-5245
www.drummondislandchamber.com

Anyone seeking a peak paddling experience might do well to consider the Drummond Island Heritage Water Trail. The island is often
touted as one of the best spots in the United States to kayak. A 60-mile,
multiday loop passes through 53 islands making up the Drummond Archipelago. Its multitude of bays and coves provide opportunities to forge
exciting explorations.

Paddlers put in at any location around the island to retrace the trav-
els of Native Americans, missionaries, French traders, and eighteenth-
century British militia. The open-water trip requires advanced paddling
skills, but those who are capable of the challenge are mightily rewarded
with breathtaking sunrises and sunsets, glorious displays of wildflowers, and viewable wildlife ranging from deer, otter, beaver, and mink to
heron, eagles, and osprey. Fossil ledges hugging the coast along Drummond's north shore and Marble Head at the isle's eastern edge are two
of Drummond's most notable natural features. Marble Head stands 100
feet above the north channel of Lake Huron. It's the only place in Michigan where the Niagara Escarpment underlying the Great Lakes is visible. Historic trail highlights include Fort Drummond, the last British
fort constructed in the United States. Built in the early 1800s to control
shipping activities, its remnants are visible from Whitney Bay. Resorts,
restaurants, and even golf opportunities allow paddlers to design the
ultimate mix of adventure and challenge without sacrificing creature
comforts.

Grand River Heritage Water Trail
Ottawa and Kent Counties
(616) 738-4810
www.miottawa.org/OC_GRHT/preferred_paddles.htm

The Grand River Heritage Water Trail is steeped in history and blessed with interesting natural features. It has 18 access points along 30 miles of the Grand River, making it possible to enjoy trips ranging from 20 minutes to 7 hours.

Meandering across mid-Michigan for 250 miles, the Grand is the longest river in the state. The designated water trail stretches from Kent County's Johnson Park to Harbor Island in Grand Haven, where the river empties into Lake Michigan. Along the route, paddlers encounter 32 historic sites, including the old Lamont Button Factory, which once produced buttons from clamshells. Paddlers also pass Stoddard Landing, the site of Ottawa County's first fruit farm and forerunner to Michigan's important fruit belt. More than 30 natural features are located along the trail. These include Kitchell Lindquist Dunes, with its rare plants and eagle population. Other lovely features explorers enjoy are patches of lotus blossoms and massive sycamore trees. The two- to three-hour paddle between Grand River Park and Eastmanville Bayou offers a serene ride down one of the longest stretches of undeveloped river frontage in Ottawa County. Crockery Creek is an hour-long out-and-back paddle. Long ago, the banks here bustled with Native American life and fur traders. If lucky, a paddler along the Grand River Trail might spot a rare American mink sliding into the water—or a fresh-faced American college student, as the trail passes through Grand Valley State University's Allendale campus.

Kalamazoo River Watershed Heritage Trail
Kalamazoo and Allegan Counties
(269) 686-9088
www.wmich.edu/glcms/watertrails/

The Kalamazoo River Watershed Heritage Trail is the first Heritage Trail to embody an entire watershed. The 162-mile-long watershed drains 10 southwest Michigan counties. In the 1800s, the Kalamazoo River was dammed at multiple points across the watershed to provide hydroelectric power. For decades, the river suffered the brunt of industrial pollution. In 2010, a major crude-oil pipeline ruptured, spilling 800,000 gallons of oil into the river near Marshall. The tragic spill served to awaken appreciation for the vital resource and spawned greater protections. Paddlers with an interest in environmental studies should note that the Morrow Dam and Power Station is the upstream boundary of the Kalamazoo River Superfund site. The site encompasses 80 miles of river from Saugatuck to 10 miles east of Battle Creek.

Despite notorious industrial abuse, the river survives as a popular paddling route. The first completed segment of the Kalamazoo River Watershed Heritage Trail opened in 2009. This segment stretches from New Richmond in Allegan County to Saugatuck. It features 18 historic sites related to lumber and the fruit industry, as well as the legendary Singapore, an abandoned coastal logging city totally buried by shifting sands. An archaeologist's delight, the lower river valley has produced artifacts from all cultural periods known in southwest Michigan. There are 13 known threatened species calling the river valley home, including the copper-bellied snake, barn owl, and Cooper's Hawk.

The Kalamazoo River's slow current makes this trail suitable for beginners. When completed, the Kalamazoo River Watershed Heritage Water Trail will stretch from the Kalamazoo River main stream in Kalamazoo to Saugatuck and feature 100 historic and natural sites.

River Country Heritage Water Trail
St. Joseph County
(800) 447-2821
www.wmich.edu/glcms/watertrails/rivercountrysj

Once a superhighway for Native Americans, the St. Joseph River now provides outdoor enthusiasts a paddle through history. St. Joseph County's nickname, River Country, stems from the fact that this southwest Michigan county features the most navigable rivers and streams in the entire state. River Country Heritage Water Trail stretches from Colon, dubbed "Home of Hocus Pocus" for its 75-year history of producing equipment for magicians, to the Village of Menden, originally the site of a Potawatomi Indian settlement. It continues on to Three Rivers, where the St. Joseph, Portage, and Rocky Rivers converge. The 210-mile-long waterway dips into Indiana for 42 miles and returns north to Michigan.

The River Country Heritage Water Trail consists of two trails along the St. Joseph and Portage Rivers and along Nottawa Creek. Paddlers of this 46-mile route may launch at most of the 37 marked sites. Historic highlights along the trail include Langley Covered Bridge, the longest of Michigan's remaining covered bridges. Markers also identify the site of the large Pottawatomi settlement, which stretched along the river bank for 12 miles. The trail weaves by the 131-year-old Rawson's King Mill. The River Country waterway also meanders through Amish country, where more than 10 percent of Michigan's Amish population lives and farms.

Plans call for the trail to eventually encompass 150 miles of this historically significant water trail.

Shiawassee River Heritage Water Trail
Oakland, Shiawassee, and Genesee Counties
(248) 634-3513
www.headwaterstrailsinc.org/shiawassee_river_trail.htm

The slow-moving, moody Shiawassee River provides both beginners and intermediate paddlers a rewarding up close and personal encounter with nature. Considered one of the best preserved warm-water river systems in the lower Great Lakes, it is renowned for its smallmouth bass population. The launch site for its easily accessed seven-mile stretch is Waterworks Park in Holly. For nearly four decades this site was the starting point for the Michigan Canoe Racing Association's first race of the season. From the trailhead at Waterworks Park, the river twists and turns through dense unspoiled natural areas to a take-out point at Fenton's Strom Park. Nine markers highlight significant features. Allow 2–3 hours for the short paddle, or 10 hours to travel the entire 35 miles currently open.

Paddling journeys provide opportunity to observe raccoon, deer, otter, heron, and eagles. The river supports 59 species of fish, 12 species of freshwater mussels, and rare species including the Indiana bat, Eastern massasauga rattlesnake, and Blanding's turtle.

Some paddling skills are needed to navigate the trail, especially at the headwaters. Paddlers might encounter a few narrow passages and an occasional beaver dam. The trail is amazingly wild, given its proximity to urban areas. Road crossings and villages are marked. Communities along the route welcome travelers. They provide respite with restaurants and shopping.

Champions of the water trail plan to install additional signage and to develop the trail another 85 miles to Saginaw Bay.

Tip of the Thumb Heritage Water Trail
Huron, Tuscola, and Sanilac Counties
info@thumbtrails.com
www.thumbtrails.com

The Tip of the Thumb Heritage Water Trail is a lighthouse lover's dream. The 139-mile water trail follows the Lake Huron coastline from Lexington in Sanilac County north to White Rock in the southeast corner of Huron County, to Harbor Beach and up to Port Austin, the midpoint. From there, it hugs the coast traveling through Saginaw Bay southward to Quanicassee in Tuscola County. The trail features 45 public launch/landing points. Route destination cities are friendly, relaxed communities and also include Port Hope, Grindstone City, Port Sanilac, Caseville, Bayport, and Sebewaing.

Historic lighthouses stand sentinel over the waterway. They include the Port Austin Reef Light, built in 1878; the Harbor Beach Lighthouse, dating back to 1885; and Pointe Aux Barques Lighthouse, near Oscabe Pointe. Campsites and picnic areas spaced along the pathway offer scenic respite stops.

Paddlers enjoy the lakeshore's diverse ecosystem and views of some of the most unique rock formations in the Great Lakes, caves, wetlands, sandy beaches, islands, and undeveloped shoreline vistas. The area provides a rich habitat for many species of protected birds and migratory waterfowl. Beadle Bay at Caseville is top bird-watching territory for cranes, egrets, eagles, and other species. Saginaw Bay is a major nesting area for migratory waterfowl and presents great opportunity for observing their annual treks through the region.

Paddlers will find a variety of conditions along this lengthy trail. They are advised to study shoreline maps before heading out and to be confident of their paddling skills.

Edgy Paddling

STAND-UP PADDLEBOARDING

Some adopt stand-up paddleboarding (SUP) for serenity or fitness, while others test their limits with an extreme version challenging the untamed Great Lakes. Michigan's fastest-growing water sport, SUP is a fusion between surfing and kayaking. It's easier than surfing and provides a birds-eye view that kayaking can't match. From their higher vantage point, paddlers are able to view swimming fish, lake bottoms, or even shipwrecks. The simplicity of the sport makes it one of the most eco-friendly water activities out there.

Depending on the waters, SUP is suitable for all ages, from children to older adults. Michigan's inland lakes provide calm surfaces to paddle and glide. The Great Lakes and rivers can offer greater challenge. Paddling hot spots include Holland, where Lake Macatawa and Lake Michigan offer distinct choices. Grand Haven and Traverse City are also popular destinations, as well as Lake Huron's Tawas Bay and Pictured Rocks National Lakeshore in the Upper Peninsula.

SUP is adaptable to your sense of adventure, as well as your fitness goals. Exercise buffs enjoy SUP as a cross-training workout. SUP yoga and Pilates are also growing in popularity. A newly formed Midwest racing circuit provides opportunities for competition. Equipment, lessons, and exercise classes are available at many of the top SUP destination communities.

FRESHWATER SURFING

Since the early 1960s, the Great Lakes surfing culture has been making quite a splash in waverider circles. Fall, winter, and spring are the best surfing seasons on the lakes when swells are most likely to be large and consistent. On average, you can expect about 10 good surfing days a month. Michigan surfing offers scores of locations to catch waves. The sites are far less crowded than ocean-surfing locations, an appealing factor to many surfers. Michigan's best breaks are found near piers, breakwalls, and points. Lake Michigan produces the most consistent waves of all the Great Lakes. Hot spots include St. Joseph, Muskegon, Grand Haven, South Haven, and points north to Leelanau County. Lake Huron provides surfing thrills from Port Austin, Port Huron, and Lexington. Lake Superior creates the highest waves and is considered by some surfers as the best lake for the freshwater version of the sport. Marquette's former zoo at Presque Isle is a prime Lake Superior destination.

Wetsuits are a must for Michigan surfers. Luckily, they're now available made from biorubber. Boards suitable for surfing the Great Lakes are available for rent and purchase at several specialty shops across the state.

Michigan surfers are on board with the eco movement. The Surfrider Foundation's Lake Michigan chapter is a grassroots environmental advocacy organization committed to protecting Great Lakes waves and beaches by increasing public awareness of environmental issues facing the inland seas.

Eco Checklist for Paddlers

Buy or rent kayaks and boards made from recycled material.
Carpool to the launch site.
Respect wildlife.
Carry out your trash.
Consider purchasing a porta-potty made especially for kayaks.
Use natural sunscreen and insect repellant.

Alvina's Betsie River

If anyone had the right to call a river her own, it was Alvina Wagner Ellis. For 78 years, Alvina defended the Upper Betsie from unsound environmental practices and served as the river's ambassador to visitors from around the globe.

Alvina first arrived in northern Michigan in the 1920s with her parents and brother. They packed a few sandwiches and a jug of coffee and made their way from Detroit in their Ford Model T along gravel roads, occasionally stopping at farmhouses for directions. The Wagners settled

beside the shores of the Betsie River at the point it meets Green Lake in
Grand Traverse County. The journey north began Alvina's lifelong mission as the river's great protector.

Alvina was a spunky, confident child. While other girls wore ankle-
length dresses, she preferred the comfort of overalls. Her playground
was the Betsie River and the wild lands surrounding the waterway. Alvina made pets of a river otter and deer. She fished and foraged, and
through the seasons developed a deep connection to nature.

It was the midst of the Great Depression when the Wagners bought
their cabin along the Upper Betsie. In those days, families made a few
dollars any way they could. Alvina's father pulled in extra cash renting
wooden boats to fishermen for 50 cents a day. For the next eight decades, Alvina was the heart and soul of the business that became known
as Alvina's Canoe and Boat Rental. The livery operated at the same site
it had since Franklin Roosevelt was president. Its original wooden boats
were replaced with canoes in the late 1960s, after the elder Wagner died.
Kayaks were later added to the little fleet. Until her death in 2013 at the
age of 93, Alvina remained steadfast in her commitment to the Betsie.
Like clockwork, she opened the livery each Memorial Day, serving as
the river's most devoted ambassador.

The Betsie originates near Interlochen and flows westerly 52 miles,
eventually reaching Lake Michigan at Frankfort. In 1973, the Betsie was
designated a state natural river to protect the waterway from development. Over the years, Alvina witnessed the river in the best of times and
the worst of times. She noted in her memoir that following World War
II, a conservation agency removed all logs from the waterway and felled
trees along the river banks to allow passage of larger recreational boats.
With its shade trees gone, the Betsie warmed. Fish populations declined
as a result.

The Betsie also fell victim to efforts to eradicate nonnative sea lam-
preys first discovered in Lake Michigan in 1936. In the 1950s, the Michigan Department of Natural Resources (DNR) used poison to rid waterways of the invasive species in hopes of protecting the Great Lakes
fishery. The chemical killed an unknown number of young pike, perch,
and bass populations. As late as 2006, news reports surfaced of lampri-
cide treatments on the Betsie inadvertently killing nontargeted fish.

In 1954, Alvina and her husband, Ralph, helped establish the Betsie River–Green Lake Association to fight state construction of the Grass Lake dam. Located four miles from Alvina's livery, the dam was part of a waterfowl- and fish-restoration effort. Despite protest, the dam was installed. After observing the project's success, the couple later fought DNR plans to remove the dam.

Alvina introduced outdoor lovers from around the world to the beauty of the Upper Betsie. Her guest book contains entries from China, Japan, Germany, Iran, Saudi Arabia, and numerous other countries. As the self-appointed river keeper, she established strict livery rules to guard the waterway from pollution. The conservationist encouraged generations of young paddlers to appreciate river wildlife by rewarding them with taffy whenever they reported seeing a beaver, heron, crane, turtle, or otter.

Alvina's unwavering commitment to safeguarding the Betsie River illustrates the power of a single individual to sustain the irreplaceable, the life-giving, the wonder-filled gifts of nature.

CHAPTER 4

Island Getaways

Take it from the birds—there's no place like an island to get away from the hustle and bustle of society. Birds flock to secluded islands for nesting and migration hiatus. So can you. As astonishing as it may seem, the Great Lakes contain more than 32,000 islands. Perch yourself on a remote isle and you just might find a new perspective on life.

The state's abundance of mostly tiny and remarkably beautiful island retreats speaks directly to the heart of any true Michigan eco-explorer. Islands offer secluded nature escapes and vast opportunities for discovery. Michigan islands provide critical habitat for waterfowl and migrating birds. Rare plants, like Pitcher's Thistle, grow here and nowhere else on earth. Fish-spawning areas and unique natural features offer vital contributions to island biodiversity.

Combined, the Great Lakes have the largest collection of freshwater islands on the planet. Isle Royale is Michigan's largest Great Lakes island. Located in the northwest corner of Lake Superior, Isle Royale is 45 miles long and 8.5 miles at its widest point. The Isle Royale National Park archipelago consists of the main island and 450 small islands. In all, the park preserves 132,000 land acres. The biodiversity of Isle Royale led to its designation in 1980 as an International Biosphere Reserve, a measure designed to balance resource use and protection of ecological integrity.

Before planning an island visit, consider what the islands are up against these days. They face threats from climate change, invasive species, residential construction, roads, and boat-access expansions. With

Fig. 4. Bicycles and carriages line the streets of the nonmotorized Mackinac Island. Six hundred horses and countless bicycles provide green transportation for thousands of island visitors. Credit: Mackinac Island Tourism Bureau.

care and thought, it's possible to enjoy island wonders without contributing to their destruction.

The listed islands restrict motorized vehicles and are easily accessed. Their infrastructure accommodates visitors while protecting ecosystems. The more curious eco-traveler may use popular island destinations as a launch point for paddling to nearby, more remote isles. Remember, there are 32,000 islands to explore—and more within Michigan's inland lakes and rivers. One calls your name.

A Classic Straits Escape

Mackinac Island
Mackinac Island Tourist Bureau
P.O. Box 451
Mackinac Island, Michigan 49757

(906) 847-6418
www.mackinawcity.com

Charm meets sustainability on Mackinac Island. Mackinac Island is celebrated by *National Geographic* and *Condé Nast Traveler* as one of the top-10 island destinations in the world. Located in Lake Huron between the Upper and Lower Peninsulas, 800,000 people make their way to the isle each year. It's clearly not a secluded destination, but when it comes to being green, Mackinac Island has a lot going for it.

From Mackinaw City the island is a 15-minute ferry ride. Ferries serving the island have a capacity of up to 400 passengers, making them a more eco-friendly transit connection than private boats, planes, or charter craft. Three companies operate regular ferry runs, providing scheduling flexibility. While the isle mostly shuts down for winter, access is possible by crossing the natural ice bridge.

Mackinac Island's great charm stems from its ability to maintain a nineteenth-century ambiance. Its restored historic buildings, narrow streets, and carless environment create a walk back in time at an easy island pace. Island transportation consists of foot traffic, bicycles, and 600 horses. The 2,200-acre island is a National Historic Landmark. Historic sites include Fort Mackinac; the British Landing, a significant War of 1812 landmark; and an 1814 battlefield. In 1875, the island was designated as the nation's second national park. Twenty years later, control was handed over to the state and it was designated Michigan's first state park.

Biking outside the tourist enclave, visitors better enjoy the island's rugged beauty. An 8-mile shoreline road and 70 miles of interior hiking/biking trails showcase towering limestone bluffs, shimmering waters, and northern woodlands.

Camping is not allowed on the island, but green lodging is available at the historic and romantic Grand Hotel. Built in 1877, the hotel earned Partner Level in the Green Lodging Michigan program for its water-based air-conditioning system and composting, and other initiatives. Half the hotel and island's waste, including horse manure, is handled by an aggressive island-wide composting program and recycling effort. Twenty-five percent of the waste stream is recycled. Twenty-five percent is composted, including yard waste. Those gorgeous island blooms you see gracing the landscape grow in island-composted material.

Legendary Lake Michigan Islands

North and South Manitou Islands
Sleeping Bear Dunes National Lakeshore
9922 Front Street
Empire, Michigan 49630
(231) 326-5134
www.nps.gov/slbe

The Manitou Islands are at the heart of a beloved legend stemming from an old Chippewa tale of a mother bear and her two cubs. The little family was forced to escape a wildfire from Wisconsin's Lake Michigan coast. Unable to swim the entire distance, the cubs died before safely reaching Michigan's shore. The Great Spirit Manitou created North and South Manitou islands to commemorate the spot the cubs drowned. The spirit created the famous Sleeping Bear Dunes to mark the place the mother bear perpetually waits for her little ones.

North and South Manitou Islands are part of Sleeping Bear Dunes National Lakeshore. The larger of the two islands, North Manitou, is located west/northwest of Leland. North Manitou is roughly 7 miles long and 4 miles wide. Although only 12 miles from the mainland, the wilderness area imparts a sense of being worlds from civilization. It offers a backcountry hiking experience with 25 miles of trails rich in opportunity for exploring open dune country, meadows, beaches, bluffs, and woodlands. North Manitou is home to the endangered Piping Plover. It also welcomes migrating geese, loons, and many other species.

To protect the fragile ecosystem and prevent introduction of invasive species, it is park practice for visitors to wipe shoes clean at the docks and to inspect clothing and gear.

Once you arrive, you can find your island happy place and set up camp. Open camping is allowed on the island's 15,000 acres, but a permit is required. Sights to explore include historic remnants. First settled in the mid-1800s, building remains and family cemeteries reflect island activity of past times.

In 1996, the National Park Service invested $190,000 to install a hybrid photovoltaic system. The seven panels generate 85 percent of the island's energy needs, decreasing the environmental risk inherent in transporting and storing fossil fuels.

South Manitou lies 16 miles west of Leland. The island features a visitor center and a lighthouse dating back to 1871. A climb to the top of the 100-foot tower offers a spectacular birds-eye look of the vast Lake Michigan. A 10-mile trail encircles the island, passing the lighthouse and a view of the wreck of the Francisco Morazan. The Valley of the Giants is located on the southwest corner of the island. This grove of virgin white cedars predates Columbus's landing in the New World.

Low-impact camping is permitted at three sites. The Bay campsites are closest to the docks. The Weather Station sites overlook Lake Michigan. It's about a three-mile hike to the more remote Popple Campground situated at the isle's northern tip. A motorized island tour is available for those unable to hike.

Transportation to both islands is provided by ferry service accessed at Leland's quaint and historic Fishtown. The ride to North Manitou is about 60 minutes. Passage to South Manitou takes about 30 minutes longer. The ferry docks at South Manitou long enough to allow day visits.

The Manitou islands provide genuine, easily accessed backcountry experiences to between 8,000 and 10,000 adventurers each year.

River Refuge

Lime Island Recreation Area
Straits State Park
720 Church Street
St. Ignace, Michigan 49781
(906) 643-8620
www.michigan.dnr.com

Powered entirely by solar panels, Lime Island is a 980-acre oasis located in the Eastern Upper Peninsula within St. Marys River Navigation Channel. The isle sits 3.5 miles from the Raber shoreline in Chippewa County. Lime Island is accessed only by private boat or charter. Paddling to the isle, while possible, is not recommended as the island sits within commercial shipping lanes.

Lime Island was once a fueling station for Great Lakes ships and supported a small village. Its visible past includes a British-era lime kiln and archeological finds dating back 4,000 years. When island commerce declined, many of its buildings were demolished. The six available rental cabins were constructed from the salvaged materials, although the cabins have since been remodeled. These simple but comfortable cabins, a caretaker cottage, outbuildings, and water pump are powered by solar panels installed on cabin roofs. Other remnants of Lime Island's heyday include a restored one-room schoolhouse and a Victorian mansion/museum. A sportsman's club operating on the isle in the 1900s attracted celebrities of the period, including Hoot Gibson, Diamond Jim Brady, and Mae West.

The island is open for fishing, hunting, hiking, and rustic camping. Ninety-five percent of the isle is covered by vegetation. Its three distinct ecosystems provide plenty of flora and fauna to discover. Wild mushrooms and asparagus are free for the picking. Deer, coyote, fox, mink, rabbits, and other small animals share the isle. Sightings of bear and moose have been reported, but are rare. Six trails weave through the island, allowing visitors to explore the high country with its maples, the pine-filled middle country, and the isle's lower cedar swamps. Perhaps the most popular island pastime is to stretch out atop the bluffs and watch freighters glide by.

Tent camping is permitted near the docks on the island's west end and at the beach at the southeast end. Both feature wooden tent platforms to reduce environmental impact. Once here, visitors find it difficult to leave the peace and quiet of this tiny river haven.

Secluded Superior Getaway

Grand Island National Recreation Area
Hiawatha National Forest Visitor Center

Munising Ranger District
400 E. Munising Avenue
Munising, Michigan 49862
(906) 387-3700

Three-hundred-foot cliffs and pristine inland waters make visiting Grand Island a memorable experience. Located about a half mile from the Munising mainland, the 13,000-acre isle is rugged, remote, and intriguing. It's accessed by ferry docks located just west of Munising, or by private boat. Tour buses are the only motorized vehicles permitted. Bike rentals are available for enjoying the island's 40 miles of dirt and sand trails. Two dedicated hiking trails provide secluded and tranquil treks. Rock hounds find happy hunting grounds at Waterfall and Mather beaches. Anglers get in on the action at Echo Beach, where trophy bass have been caught at the catch-and-release lake. The lake was created by beavers and is the largest social lake (that is, one created by social animals) in the nation.

Overnighters may choose random camping or the better eco-choice of setting up camp at one of 17 designated campsites located at three sites: Murray Bay, Juniper Flats, and Trout Bay. Trout Bay is favored by anglers for snagging lake trout and Coho. The rich island fishery also includes perch, pike, walleye, bass, and pan fish. Dramatic views of Pictured Rocks National Lakeshore are seen from Trout Bay shores.

Visitors traveling from the docking area at Williams Landing to Murray Bay pass a number of aged buildings, relics of a resort development. Island historical landmarks include farm fields once cultivated by early fur traders. These fields are part of a native-plant restoration project forwarded by Superior Watershed Partnership and the Hiawatha National Forest. Between 2008 and 2010, 77,000 native plants were planted here. Each was grown from seed harvested in the Hiawatha National Forest. The reintroduction of native plants provides critical habitat for pollinators, birds, and wildlife. Restoration plantings include milkweed, black-eyed Susans, coreopsis, verbain, and others. The fields provide a colorful show of blooms between late June and early August. Handcrafted benches afford visitors the opportunity to rest and take in the native-plant garden's beauty.

Grand Island is also a prime winter destination for ice climbing. A hike across the frozen Munising Bay to the isle's northern shore provides access to dramatic curtains of ice formed along the island's sandstone cliffs. Climbing typically begins mid-December. The Munising area is considered one of the nation's premier ice-climbing centers. Frozen waterfalls form towers 20–200 feet tall. Favorite climbs are found along Sand Point Road and at Miners Falls. Munising celebrates the sport each February with the Michigan Ice Fest. The event features professional climbers, demonstrations, and clinics to introduce future climbers to the ins and outs of the sport.

Only 10 minutes from the mainland, Grand Island is a Lake Superior treasure and undoubtedly one of the Upper Peninsula's most beautiful places to enjoy four seasons of sustainable adventures.

Eco Checklist for Island Adventures

Is eco-friendly transportation available to and from the island?
Is motorized traffic prohibited?
How is island waste managed?
Is new construction and growth on the island managed in accordance to sustainable practices?
Are alternative forms of energy available?
Is green lodging available?
Are sensitive island ecosystems protected?

Island of Genius

Long before the environmental movement began, some of the greatest minds of the twentieth century found inspiration on a tiny secluded island situated in West Grand Traverse Bay. Today the island is owned by Grand Traverse County. Visitors can stroll the same sandy shores and hardwood forests where legendary figures shared innovative ideas, fellowship, and good times. Located only two miles from the Bowers Harbor public launch on Old Mission Peninsula, Power Island is easily accessed by kayak, either paddler-owned or rented from local liveries.

Between 1917 and 1944, this 200-acre isle was owned by American industrialist and founder of the Ford Motor Company, Henry Ford. Ford traveled to the island via yacht, bringing an entourage of friends and dignitaries to his private retreat. Visitors included baseball icon Babe Ruth, auto pioneers the Dodge and Olds brothers, and Harvey Firestone, founder of Firestone Tire and Rubber Company. Three U.S. presidents joined the island visitor list, including Warren Harding, Woodrow Wilson, and Teddy Roosevelt, as well as Ford's great pal, inventor Thomas Edison.

Ford, Edison, Firestone, and literary naturalist John Burroughs had a tradition of camping together. Known as the Four Vagabonds, they began a series of camping excursions in 1914. According to Henry Ford Estate archives, their "gypsy" trips signified the "first linking of cars with outdoor recreation." Burroughs, a forerunner of the modern conservation movement, noted in his journal how the foursome hungered for outdoor experiences. He wrote, they "cheerfully endure wet, cold, smoke, mosquitoes, black flies, and sleepless nights, just to touch naked reality once more."

These big thinkers proved that all work and no play wasn't their style. Camping beneath the stars, Ford was no stranger to chopping firewood and flipping pancakes. Local legend recounts how when Ford wanted to throw a dance on his island, Edison's genius was applied to providing lighting for the event. Guests partied into the night thanks to the inventor's idea to rig a generator to bicycles as a means to create electricity for dance floor lights.

The island's original owner purchased the isle in 1881, naming it after his daughter, Marion. The island's current name, Power Island, was bestowed on the isle after the passing of its last private owner, Eugene Power of Ann Arbor. But this isle by any name is a sweet experience. Walk where the great minds of modern society walked. Gaze at the skies from the places they contemplated pivotal world events. Ponder the mysteries of the universe around a blazing campfire, as they did. Eleven miles of hiking trails meander through island woodlands. Birds and bobcat, deer, raccoon, and fox roam its hilled terrain.

A causeway, accessible during low water periods, links Power Island's northeast tip to the two-acre Bassett Island. Bassett Island has its own colorful past. It was once known as Haunted Island. The name arose from the legend of a young girl left stranded on the isle. Civil War veteran and hermit David Bassett purchased the mini isle in the late 1800s. In 1901, the isle was turned into a tourist attraction after it was purchased by a steamship company which constructed a dance pavilion on the island for pleasure travelers.

The Grand Traverse County Parks and Recreation Department maintains five rustic campsites on Bassett Island. Each has a picnic table, cooking grill, and campfire circle. There is a fee for camping, but anyone can visit both islands free of charge. Quite a bargain for the opportunity to stand in the footprints of genius.

CHAPTER 5

Wildlife Connections

G et your Davey Crockett on and prepare to explore the Mitten State's amazing wildlife. From giant moose to soaring falcons, connect to Michigan's animal kingdom sharing the great peninsulas with us. A good pair of walking shoes, some binoculars, and a camera are all you need to forge a compelling wildlife experience amongst the natural habitats of native birds and animals.

We can learn a lot from observing our animal neighbors. They show us how perfectly nature provides for our needs, how important it is to be aware of the surrounding environment, the role of interdependence, and that it is the wise individual who knows how to let instinct guide.

The better we understand the lives of Michigan's animals, the better chance we have at protecting them and their habitats under threat from encroachment, invasive species, pollution, and the impact of global warming.

It is no longer possible to ignore the toll climate change imposes on Michigan's animals. Like a modern-day Grim Reaper, the record-high temperatures and dry summer of 2012 are believed to have led to the death of up to 50,000 Michigan white-tailed deer. Considered the worst deer kill in the state's history, the Michigan Department of Natural Resources reported the summer's weather conditions resulted in an outbreak of the fatal virus epizootic hemorrhagic disease (EHD). The EHD outbreak occurred primarily in Michigan's central and southern counties. Ionia County experienced the greatest official loss of any county with the death of 2,450 deer.

In most years, a herd of about 1 million deer roam Michigan, a state with a grand variety of creatures—691 animal species in all. Its geo-

Fig. 5. Nine hundred elk roam free in the Pigeon River Country State Forest. Michigan's herd nearly disappeared in the 1800s. It was reestablished from seven animals relocated to Cheboygan County in 1918. Credit: Pam Duczkowski.

graphic location within the Great Lakes makes it an important flyway attracting a rich diversity of wildlife, especially waterfowl. Each year, Michigan hosts visits from more than 3 million migrating waterfowl.

Photography adds a layer of interest to any wildlife excursion. It's a thrill to capture a shot of a rare bird or spotted fawn in their natural environment. Successfully shooting bird and animal photos requires an understanding of an animal's routines and habitats and the ability to cloak ourselves within the surroundings. Patience and timing make the magic happen. It also takes forethought to be at the right place at the right time whether photographing elk during mating season or snowy owls in winter. For those who enjoy adding a touch of creativity to the eco-experience, wildlife photography can be highly rewarding.

While the opportunity to view wildlife provides engaging experiences, education, and recreation, sustainability requires we give full respect to the creatures we hope to encounter. Follow park or preserve guidelines. Have fun. Expand your understanding and share your experiences.

To the Bat Cave

Millie Mine
Park Avenue off A Street
Iron Mountain, Michigan 49801
(800) 236-2447

Tippy Dam
1325 Tippy Dam Road
Wellston, Michigan 49689
(231) 848-4411

Whether you love or fear bats, you have to agree they're fascinating creatures. Michigan is a bat haven, harboring one of the largest-known clusters of bats in the Midwest. If bat watching intrigues you, there's opportunity aplenty.

The Upper Peninsula's mineral-mining industry of the past two centuries unknowingly contributed to the preservation of the bat population. After mining's decline, thousands of abandoned mine shafts were adopted by bats for roosting and hibernation. About 30 of these sites are protected with special grates to allow for safe public viewing of the bat's nightly routine.

Millie Mine, near Iron Mountain, is a hibernating and breeding spot for as many as 50,000 bats that migrate there from throughout the Great Lakes region. While Michigan is home to nine bat species, it's primarily big brown and little brown bats that favor the Millie Mine. They arrive and settle into the mine between late August and early September and reappear in April. Prime viewing time is September through early October at dusk when they emerge from the deep shaft to feed. Millie Mine features a bat interpretive center and has served as the host location for a national bat festival presented by Bat Conservation International.

Bats and corporate Michigan continue to have a positive relationship in present times. Consumers Energy operates Tippy Hydro, a hydroelectric dam spanning the Manistee River in Manistee County. Tippy's spillway provides a cozy spot for 24,000 hibernating bats. Four species are known to hibernate within the cavernous structure, including the endangered Indiana bat. Located near Wellston, the site has attracted bats since constructed in 1918 and is the largest bat "cave" in the Lower Peninsula.

General Motors (GM) and bats seem an unlikely association, but the global auto maker is going green by providing bat housing in Detroit. GM environmental engineers work with community groups to convert used Chevrolet Volt battery covers into bat houses rather than send the material to a landfill. The houses made from recycled material are installed at area wildlife habitats.

The Monarch's Epic Migration

Hiawatha National Forest
Rapid River Ranger District
499 East Lake Shore Drive
Manistique, Michigan 49854
(906) 341-5666
www.fs.usda.gov/hiawatha

Tawas Point State Park
686 Tawas Beach Road
East Tawas, MI 48730
(989) 362-5041
www.michigandnr.com/parksandtrails

Holland State Park
2215 Ottawa Beach Road
Holland, Michigan 49424
(616) 399-9390
www.michigandnr.com/parksandtrails

Imagine tens of thousands of Monarch butterflies filling the sky with their brilliant-colored wings. This spectacle draws butterfly enthusiasts from across the country to prime migration viewing spots along Michigan's Great Lakes.

In August and September, the Upper Peninsula's Delta County becomes the butterfly capital of Michigan. Clouds of Monarch butterflies gather along Stonington Peninsula at Peninsula Point Lighthouse Park to rest before continuing their annual flight from Canada to wintering grounds in Mexico. Look for butterflies roosting in the park's cedar trees, where they seek protection from the elements. Lake Michigan serves as a map for the Monarch's journey. From the Upper Peninsula they travel to Wisconsin's Door Peninsula and proceed to south of the border. The journey is one of more than 2,000 miles for some of these delicate creatures.

Tawas Point State Park in Iosco County is another prime location for witnessing the Monarch pageant along Michigan's eastern coastline. The sandy peninsula protrudes into Lake Huron, attracting not only butterflies but up to 200 species of migratory birds.

The million-Monarch epic migration may also be witnessed at Holland State Park in Ottawa County.

Moose Safari

Seney National Wildlife Refuge
1674 Refuge Entrance Road
Seney, Michigan 49883
(906) 586-9851
www.fws.gov/midwest/seney

Tahquamenon Falls State Park
41382 West M-123

Paradise, Michigan 49768
(906) 492-3415
www.michigandnr.com/parksandtrails

Van Riper State Park
851 County Road AKE
Champion, Michigan 49814
(906) 339-4461
www.michigandnr.com/parksandtrails

You don't have to travel farther than the Upper Peninsula to view large animals in the wild. To say it's a thrill to witness a 1,500-pound moose lumbering through the forest is an understatement. Thanks to concerted conservation efforts, the experience is more than a distant possibility for adventurers willing to take a trek through Michigan moose country.

A member of the deer family and native to Michigan, moose were wiped out in the Lower Peninsula by 1900. The Upper Peninsula herd was drastically thinned by loggers, miners, and settlers who relied on moose for sustenance. In the mid-1980s, an effort was made to rebuild the Upper Peninsula population with 59 animals relocated from Ontario, Canada. The herd increased over the years. The free-ranging moose herd now consists of about 500 animals who roam at will across Michigan terrain.

There are three viewing hot spots in the Upper Peninsula. They include Van Riper State Park, near Champion; Seney National Wildlife Refuge at Seney; and Tahquamenon Falls State Park, near Newberry. In 2002, the Michigan legislature deemed Newberry, located in Luce County, the Moose Capital of Michigan. Newberry claims more moose sightings than anywhere else in Michigan, making it a good place to begin a moose safari.

Hiking is the primary means to catch sight of this impressive animal. Park staff is able to offer information on recent sightings and local herd movement. Moose feed on water plants during the summer months and so may be found frequenting ponds, lakes, streams, and marshes. A quest for the big one may also provide encounters with other native wildlife, as moose share habitat with bear, deer, foxes, and wolves.

Elk Pursuits

Pigeon River Country State Forest
(989) 983-4101
www.michigan.gov/elk

City of Gaylord Elk Park
East Grandview
Gaylord, Michigan 49735
(800) 345-8621
www.gaylordmichigan.net/elk-viewing—40/

Thunder Bay Resort
27800 M-32
Hillman, Michigan 49746
(800) 729-9375
www.thunderbayresort.com

The elk's haunting call reverberating through the wilds stirs something primal within a person's soul. Pigeon River Country State Forest is where the Michigan eco-explorer is most likely to catch sight of elk and hear the voice of this mighty beast. The 100,000-acre Pigeon River State Forest is home to 900 elk. Weighing up to 1,000 pounds, males sport antlers topping the scales at 40 pounds. These native giants bugle, breed, feed, give birth, and raise young within the forest's rolling hills, lakes, open lands, and secluded bogs. As a result of the Michigan Department of Natural Resources' (DNR) wildlife management and conservation efforts, the herd is the largest free-roaming herd east of the Mississippi. But in 1875, the elk had nearly vanished. To rebuild the population, in 1918 seven elk were relocated from the western United States to the wilds near Wolverine, located in Cheboygan County. Pigeon River Country's herd is descended from those transplants.

The DNR provides a downloadable map (www.michigan.gov/docu ments/dnr/DNR_Elk_Brochure_401828_7.pdf) detailing the 11 designated elk-viewing spots in Cheboygan and Otsego Counties most likely to provide sightings. Sites are accessed by seasonal roads, but some call for a short trek into the elk habitat. The most popular period for spotting elk is September during the rut season when the animals are most active. While elk may be spotted during daylight hours, dusk and dawn are considered prime viewing time.

For a tamer elk experience, visit Gaylord's City Elk Park. The city cares for a herd of about 70 elk, which freely roam on 108 acres. The park was established more than 14 years ago following the closing of a nearby nature center. The family-friendly viewing area is easily accessed. Gaylord's animals are curious about their visitors and provide great photo opportunities.

Elk viewing takes an old-fashioned twist at Thunder Bay Resort in Hillman. Carriages and sleighs pulled by Percheron horses travel through the woods and across Thunder Bay River in pursuit of the beasts. It's a charming way to view springtime's newborn calves or autumn's bugling males. A Michigan Green Lodging applicant, the resort offers other experiences celebrating simplicity, like gourmet meals cooked on antique woodstoves. Onsite trails offer hiking, biking, cross-country skiing, and snowshoeing for additional low-impact fun.

Urban Wilds

Detroit River International Wildlife Refuge
Large Lakes Research Station
9311 Groh Road
Grosse Ile, Michigan 48138
(734) 692-7608
http://www.fws.gov/refuge/detroit_river/

Urban birding in Michigan is not only possible—its unique opportunities are recognized worldwide. The Detroit River International Wildlife Refuge received official designation in 2001. The first International Wildlife Refuge in North America, it sits 20 miles south of Detroit in the midst of an urban population of 6 million people. Situated along the lower Detroit River and western Lake Erie, the refuge's 6,000 acres encompass a diversity of habitats including coastal wetlands, marshes, shoals, islands, and waterfront land stretching for 48 miles.

The age of industrialization took a heavy toll on this ecosystem, but concerted restoration efforts spanning three decades are writing a new story. The refuge is cited as one of the most successful restoration projects in the country and a premier birding site. Sitting at the junction of the Atlantic and Mississippi flyways, the southeast Michigan wildlife haven hosts a phenomenal array of feathered visitors. Overall, the habitat hosts more than 300 bird species. More than 300,000 ducks rest and feed here during migration, as well as 75,000 shorebirds and 100,000 hawks. The lower Detroit River is recognized as one of the top spots in North America for observing hawks during the autumn raptor migration. Migratory journeys are celebrated each fall with Hawkfest, held at Lake Erie Metropark, a prime viewing spot for migrating hawks, eagles, falcons, owls, and vultures.

The Detroit River refuge offers birders multiple options for wildlife watching. A trail and observation platform are located at the 410-acre Humbug Marsh. Humbug Marsh is the state's only Wetlands of International Importance designated under the Ramsar Convention intergovernmental treaty protecting waterfowl habitat. The marsh features the sole remaining mile of untouched Detroit River shoreline along the U.S. mainland. The 44-acre refuge gateway marks the reserve's entry. Formerly owned by Chrysler, the property is now owned by Wayne County. Plans call for establishing a visitor center at the gateway to serve as a model for sustainable living.

"Byways to Flyways," a downloadable brochure, highlights 27 top birding points across the Windsor-Detroit region. It includes 8 highly significant observation spots. Download it free at http://www.mac-web .org/Projects/DiscoverOurWildSide/BywaysToFlyways.htm.

Surprisingly, birding isn't limited to the wilds surrounding Detroit. Downtown Detroit is an unlikely but good viewing spot for peregrine falcons. Falcons are seen swooping and sailing above Motown streets, diving for prey at extreme speeds. Nighthawks and swallows are also commonly spotted in Michigan urban environments.

Birds Galore

Shiawassee National Wildlife Refuge
6975 Mower Road
Saginaw, Michigan 48601
(989) 777-5930
http://www.fws.gov/refuge/shiawassee/

If you can imagine 50,000 waterfowl congregating in one place, you can imagine Shiawassee National Wildlife Refuge. A squawking orchestra of transient creatures fills this massive wetland with the sound of life. During peak migration periods, 20,000 Canada geese and 30,000 ducks congregate to feed and rest within the preserve's 9,000 acres. Shiawassee National Wildlife Refuge ranks among America's top 25 birding areas.

Located with the Saginaw Bay watershed, Shiawassee Flats, as it is commonly called, is one of the largest wetland ecosystems in the state. The refuge, Shiawassee River State Game Area, and Green Point Environmental Learning Center jointly provide access to this diverse and fascinating habitat, where nearly 400 species of migratory birds and songbirds are found. Shore birds, wading birds, raptors, warblers, heron, and others can be spotted. Deer, otter, beaver, fox, turtles, and other creatures are also encountered at the Flats.

Exploration is facilitated by more than 10 miles of year-round trails open for low-impact adventuring via hiking, biking, and cross-country skiing. The Ferguson Bayou Trail features three observation decks. Two provide spotting scopes. The learning center allows for wildlife viewing from within the facility. Prime viewing months are March and April, and October and November.

The vibrancy and diversity of Shiawassee Flats creates appreciation for the importance and beauty of wetland areas. It's a true masterpiece exhibiting Mother Nature's capacity to balance the complex fabrics of life.

Eco Checklist for Wildlife Watching

Keep at least 100 yards between you and wildlife.

Resist feeding wildlife to avoid dependence on humans.
Keep pets leashed to prevent confrontations.
Never chase wildlife.
Avoid nesting areas, dens, and rookeries.
Learn and follow rules established by park management or other
   authorities.

Where Wolves Roam

The remarkable comeback of Michigan's gray wolf population exempli-
fies humankind's ability to destroy and protect, as well as nature's recu-
perative capacity.

Wolves were doomed from the moment the Puritans stepped foot in
the New World. As early as the 1600s, Massachusetts colonists placed
bounties on the heads of these pack animals. In 1838, Michigan's first
legislature created a wolf bounty as the state's ninth law.

Prior to the state's settlement, wolves roamed each of Michigan's 83
counties surviving on deer, beaver, raccoon, other small mammals, insects, berries, and nuts. Whether it was perceived or real, wolves were a
great enough menace to the state's settlers that some communities paid
wolf-slayers cash above the state bounty. The cash-for-scalps program
quickly wiped out Michigan's gray wolves. In Saginaw County, for example, wolf-slayers were paid $8 per scalp. Ten years later, hardly a wolf
remained within the entire county.

The state law remained on the books until 1960, with the exception
of a short period in the early 1900s in which trapping laws were in effect.
By 1910, wolves had vanished from the Lower Peninsula. And by 1973,
only six wolves were estimated to remain. These roamed the remote Isle
Royale Island in the Upper Peninsula.

The decimation and later recovery of the wolf population is linked
to societal attitudes toward the natural environment, according to the
Michigan Department of Natural Resources' (DNR) wolf-management-
plan document. The document explains that until the late 1800s, the
wild lands and their creatures were viewed as entities to be tamed, con-
trolled, and dominated. Preservation advocacy developed when people
understood nature is a limited resource, and sport hunters began to

promote wildlife management. Favored species first gained protection, while predatory animals, such as wolves, continued to have bounties on their heads.

The tides changed for Michigan wolves in 1965 when the state granted them full legal protection. The gray wolf was listed as a threatened and endangered species in 1974 under the federal Endangered Species Preservation Act.

After an unsuccessful attempt to introduce new wolves to the Michigan population, the DNR let nature take its course. Wolves migrated to the Upper Peninsula from Minnesota, Wisconsin, and Ontario. In 1992, the wolf population had expanded from 6 to 21 animals. A significant comeback was underway.

Just as the wolf's demise is attributed to public attitudes, so is their recovery. DNR surveys conducted in the mid-1990s showed broad public acceptance of the wolf. In the same decade, an annual Michigan Wolf Awareness Week was established and a Michigan Gray Wolf Recovery Team appointed. In 2008, a state wolf-management plan emphasized the coexistence of wolves and humans.

Controversy brewed as wolf packs grew. In 2007, Michigan wolves were removed from the federal list of threatened and endangered species. The ruling was overturned by a federal court and they were relisted. In 2009, wolves again lost protection status. Two months later the delisting was rejected due to procedural technicalities.

By 2012, the Upper Peninsula's wolf population reached 700, exceeding federal recovery goals. Finally, on January 27, 2012, wolves were officially removed from the federal endangered-species list and management authority was placed with the DNR.

Despite opposition, decades of effort to restore the wolf population hit a serious snag in July 2013 when under a new law the Michigan Natural Resources Commission named the wolf a game species, allowing for a public wolf hunt. Michigan's wolf season was set for November 15 through December 31, and a total of 1,200 licenses were made available for the harvest of 43 animals from Upper Peninsula public and private lands. The hunt was to continue until the quota was met.

Without federal protection, the wolf's future in Michigan dims, even if it's not doomed, and the saga of the state's wolf population continues.

CHAPTER 6

The Green Golfer

Border to border, golf courses are an integral part of the Michigan landscape. With more than 850 public courses, Michigan has a greater number of places to play the game than any other state.

Accolades for Michigan courses roll in each year. Four are ranked among the nation's top 100 by industry experts. For golfers, that's good news. For environmentalists, the proliferation of courses is a worrisome matter. Fortunately, a shift toward sustainable golf course management is underway.

Golf's reputation as an environmental foe is well based. The manicured greens golfers prize come at an ecological price. Courses annually apply on average 12 pounds of pesticides per acre. In many instances, poundage exceeds that applied per acre by farmers. Water conservationists wring their hands because a single course's water use on average equals the water required to support a town of 8,000.

When the game was invented 600 years ago, it was played amidst natural settings in the Scottish hills. Until the post–World War II era, most courses followed suit and were developed by conforming to the features of the land. Technological advances and irrigation opened later development to almost any location. As a result, natural habitats were destroyed to make way for the game, wildlife displaced, and natural vegetation replaced by unnatural turf.

Economics defined by tough fiscal times have ushered in new practices in the world of golf. Courses began to struggle with the high cost of maintaining picture-perfect greens under financial, ecological, and social pressure. What are emerging are efforts to raise the bar on envi-

Fig. 6. Native landscaping graces fairways at Forest Dunes Golf Club in Roscommon. Forest Dunes is the sixth course in the world to earn Audubon International Gold certification for adherence to sustainable management principles. Credit: Forest Dunes Golf Club.

ronmentally sound management, and a breed of golfer who understands the spirit of the game is intimately linked to the vibrancy of nature.

Michigan golf courses step up their game by embracing innovation and commitment in the pursuit of sustainability. The golfer may gauge a course's green progress by various course certifications. Endorsed by the United States Golf Association, the Audubon Cooperative Sanctuary Program for Golf recognizes courses that successfully adapt preservation practices. The program focuses on enhancing course natural areas and minimizing harmful impacts. Certification requires completing eco-friendly practices in environmental planning, wildlife and habitat management, outreach and education, chemical use reduction and safety, water conservation, and water quality management.

Course greens are more significant to the big eco-picture than one might think. Turfgrass covers 5 percent of Michigan's total land. It includes golf courses, schools, parks, and cemeteries. The Michigan Turfgrass Environmental Stewardship Program promotes awareness of the state's natural resources, the positive potential of golf turf management, and pollution protection. It was developed at Michigan State University with support from the Michigan Turfgrass Association, the Golf Association of Michigan, the Michigan Department of Environmental Quality, and the Michigan Department of Agriculture. Courses enrolled in the Turfgrass Stewardship Program show commitment to improving environmental factors.

Golf Environment Organization (GEO) is an international nonprofit dedicated to advancing sustainability in golf around the globe. Although only a handful of U.S. courses have earned certification, the organization is represented in Michigan and provides an internationally recognized eco-golf program. Certification criteria address landscapes and ecosystems, water usage, energy and resources, products, and supply chains.

In this age of climate change, the golfer's responsibility in greening the game is to understand the ecological impact of the courses he or she chooses to play. By expressing support for sustainable facilities, choosing recyclable balls, biodegradable tees, or other equipment, the player makes an important contribution in establishing a new low-impact golf ethic.

Eco-Friendly Fairways
Forest Dunes Golf Club
6376 Forest Dunes Drive
Roscommon, Michigan 48653
(989) 275-0700
www.forestdunesgolf.com

The Forest Dunes property has been singled out for the past century for its secluded location. A storied history follows it through the decades. Forest Dunes was once owned by General Motors founder William Durant. In the 1930s, Durant sold a portion of the land to Detroit underworld figures for a recreation center. Forest Dunes made eco history in 2003 when it became the sixth course in the world to earn Audubon International Gold Signature certification. One year later, Forest Dunes achieved Michigan Turfgrass Environmental Stewardship certification.

When the 18-hole Tom Weiskopf Signature Course was developed in 1997, the first step was to conduct a comprehensive inventory of plants, animals and insects, soil and groundwater. Seed was harvested during construction, grown in greenhouses, and planted at the site. Not only is Forest Dunes recognized as a top 100 public course in America, it leads the pack in environmentally sound practices. Resource management includes use of low-impact chemicals and organic fertilizers, and minimum irrigation practices. Pesticide use is limited to curative purposes and regular water testing is conducted to ensure water quality protection.

The destination course is surrounded by the million-acre Huron National Forest. The course's front nine holes offer traditional Michigan golf amidst wooded scenery. The back nine features a wide open layout with pristine views, dunes, and tall grasses. Forest Dunes includes a total of 25 acres of native grass. While only 80 acres are maintained as turf, the course is interesting and offers enjoyable play.

Fox Hills Golf & Banquet Center
8768 North Territorial Road
Plymouth, Michigan 48170
(734) 453-7272
www.foxhills.com

Offering 63 holes for play, Fox Hills is the largest golf facility in southeast Michigan. The family-owned club dates back to the early 1900s. Their vision for sustainability sprouted long before the environmental movement was born, giving Fox Hills nearly two decades of eco-friendly practices under its belt. In 1996, Fox Hills became the third Michigan course to earn Audubon Cooperative Sanctuary certification. It's also a member of the Turfgrass Environmental Stewardship Program. In 2002, Fox Hills was named the National Course of the Year by the National Golf Course Owners Association for overall management practices, programs, and environmental practices. More accolades came in 2008 when the course was recognized by Washtenaw County with its Water Quality Award.

Eco-friendly measures at Fox Hills include conversion of more than 28 acres of turf to natural areas or grass, and the planting of trees, shrubs, and wetland vegetation. It added buffer zones to reduce chemical runoff, and installed bat houses to biologically control insects. Working with local elementary students, 78 bird nesting boxes were installed to help restore bluebird populations.

Fox Hills features three distinct courses: the Golden Fox, Fox Classic, and the Strategic Fox. Course diversity allows golfers of all skill levels to experience a challenging game.

Gull Lake View Golf Resort
7417 North 38th Street
Augusta, Michigan 49012
(269) 731-4149
www.gulllakeview.com

Dr. Jane Goodall, one of the planet's most renowned animal researchers, presented Gull Lake Golf Resort the Community Environmental Leadership Award on behalf of the Kalamazoo Nature Center. Since earning the recognition in 2000, Gull Lake has continued to work hand in hand with the nature center toward natural resource protection. Gull Lake and the nature center collaborated to create a Blue Bird Trail throughout the resort's five courses. The project also recorded, banded, and fledged thousands of bluebirds. Each of Gull Lake's courses is certified in the Audubon Cooperative Sanctuary and Michigan Turfgrass Environmental Stewardship programs.

Gull Lake applies a holistic philosophy to management. The resort has reduced water use, reduced waste, managed energy consumption, and protected water quality. It applies the same sustainable principles to its planned communities, setting aside 50 percent of the land as green space.

Gull Lake is southwest Michigan's oldest and largest golf resort. Its 18-hole championship courses include Gull Lake View East, Gull Lake View West, Stonehedge North, Stonehedge South, and Bedford Valley.

Bedford Valley hosted the Michigan Open, the Michigan Senior Open, the Michigan Maxfli PGA Junior Championship, the Michigan Publinx State Match Play, and the NCAA III National Championship. From dramatic elevation changes, to natural water hazards and undulating greens, the golf community is offered a rich diversity of courses to test their skills.

Harbor Shores Golf Club
201 Graham Avenue
Benton Harbor, Michigan 49022
(269) 927-4653
www.harborshoreslife.com

Legendary golfers Arnold Palmer, Johnny Miller, Tom Watson, and Jack Nicklaus competed in the Harbor Shores Golf Club opening event in 2010. Two years later, the 18-hole, Nicklaus-designed course hosted the 2012 Senior PGA Championship and was on tap to host the event in 2014. But this rising star of the golf universe is most remarkable for the fact it transformed a toxic industrial waste site into a productive recreational asset. Hole 15 is a former Superfund Site, while hole 14 was a city landfill, and hole 16 was an industrial dumping ground. In all, 117,000 tons of trash, solid waste, and concrete and 20,000 tons of contaminated soil were removed to create the course.

Winding through woods, dunes, and wetlands, the Nicklaus Signature Course is designed to prevent runoff into the water table and ecologically sensitive wetlands. Each hole is named for a native plant, raising player awareness of the local habitat. Three holes provide views of the shimmering Lake Michigan. With four sets of tees, the course is playable for all skill levels. Harbor Shores is also home to the Midwest's first Jack Nicklaus Academy of Golf.

Radrick Farms Golf Course
4875 Geddes Road
Ann Arbor, Michigan 48105
(734) 998-7040
www.radrick.umich.edu

The University of Michigan's Radrick Farms Golf Course has forwarded a vision of stewardship since the 1930s when the original property owner, Frederick Matthaei Sr., farmed the land. Matthaei, an alumnus and former regent, grew one of every indigenous Michigan tree on the property, which he eventually donated to the university.

Opened in the mid-1960s, the Radrick Farms course is an early design of famed course architect Peter Dye. The 18-hole championship layout incorporates 109 of the property's 275 acres. Radrick Farms Golf Course is certified in both the Audubon Cooperative Sanctuary and Michigan Turfgrass Environmental Stewardship programs. It is the only Michigan course participating in the Groundwater Guardian Green Site Program, an initiative advocating groundwater-friendly practices at highly managed green spaces.

Radrick Farms collaborates with multiple community organizations to promote environmental goals. Partners include the Community Partners for Clean Streams, a Washtenaw County initiative protecting waterways from pollution; the Matthaei Botanical Gardens; and the Dundee Chapter of Future Farmers of America.

Facility managers implement modern technology for maintaining course quality and achieving ecological benefits. Moisture meters, infrared thermometers, compaction meters, and other instruments provide data for applying best practices in chemical and water use. Fifty-eight percent of the waste generated at Radrick Farms is recycled.

The secluded private course has an open to the public guest policy. Its rolling terrain features 100 acres of mixed forest. The artfully designed, tree-lined fairways provide a rewarding experience and peace of mind in knowing that sustainability and golf coexist.

Tournament Players Club
One Nicklaus Drive
Dearborn, Michigan 48120
(313) 436-3000
www.tpcofmichigan.com

Dearborn's Tournament Players Club (TPC) was the first golf course honored with the John James Audubon Environmental Steward Award for ecological restoration. Established in 1990, the course occupies a 212-acre site originally purchased by Henry Ford. Located within the River Rouge floodplain, the property was a dump site before its transformation to a community asset. Construction workers unearthed all manner of manufacturing waste during the restoration process. The private club's course was designed by Jack Nicklaus, with Audubon International guidelines in mind. Massive plantings helped restore natural habitats, while enhancing aesthetics. The club maintains the course with respect for wildlife and in accordance to sustainability practices. Daily monitoring of the greens reduces TPC's watering by 30 percent. Pesticides and fertilizers are used sparingly.

The par 72, links-style course stretches across scenic rolling hills. It is known for hosting the Ford Senior Players Championship for 16 years. *Golfweek* and *Golf Digest* rate TPC "Best in Michigan."

Eco Checklist for Golf Courses

What are the course's water-quality management practices?
How does the course handle plant management?
How does the course approach wildlife and habitat management?
Does course design and siting lend itself to sustainability?
Is integrated pest management practiced?
How are energy and waste managed?
Are affiliated restaurants, hotels, and other operations green?

Earth Keepers

In 2003, the Grand Traverse Band of Ottawa & Chippewa Indians acquired the Grand Traverse Resort and Spa, along with its three signature golf courses. It was only 23 years earlier that the band received federal recognition and it had quickly grown into a major economic force within northwest Michigan. In 1984, the band opened Leelanau Sands Casino, a move marking it as one of the first tribes in the United States to run a casino.

The Grand Traverse Band of Ottawa & Chippewa Indians remains a primary employer in the region, with an annual payroll of $19.8 million (2010). It works with 900 regional and state vendors, purchasing $17.8 million in goods and services each year. As financially savvy as the tribe has proven itself, this sovereign nation approaches business and life from a different perspective than traditional American companies.

Members of the Grand Traverse Band of Ottawa & Chippewa Indians are among the indigenous Anishinaabe peoples. Teachings passed down through the generations call for the Anishinaabeg to care for Mother Earth and to honor all living things. The tribe considers it their duty to infuse its spiritual philosophies into all life matters, including the golf courses in their possession.

The resort's three 18-hole golf courses, The Bear, The Wolverine, and Spruce Run, are among the nation's premier golf facilities. Designed by the industry's leading course architects, the facilities are highly praised. But these outstanding courses earn recognitions many players may never know.

After the purchase, it became the tribe's mission to honor the resort's 900 acres and all it contains. While golfers racked up wins on the fairways, the Anishinaabeg earth keepers pursued other victories. In 1997, they achieved certification as a Cooperative Sanctuary by Audubon International. The following year they garnered the Golf Course Superintendents Association of America Environmental Steward Award. The Michigan Turfgrass Environmental Stewardship certification was achieved in 2006. The facility was more recently lauded by the Environmental Institute for Golf.

Earth keeping is a far-reaching activity for the band. Resort management pursued Leader certification for its 600-room hotel through Green Lodging Michigan. The voluntary program created by the Michigan Department of Labor and Economic Growth requires adoption of practices pertaining to energy conservation, air quality, and reduced consumption and waste.

In 2008, the tribe constructed an all-new Turtle Creek Casino and Hotel in Williamsburg. They kept the project in the Michigan "family," ensuring 80 percent of the $115 million project was spent in the state. The casino/hotel was built green from the bottom up, topped with a living roof of hostas, ferns, and daylilies. It was the first casino in Michigan, and one of a handful of buildings overall, to install the eco-friendly crown. But Turtle Creek's eco-beauty is more than skin deep. Even the casino's 1,300 slots are eco-friendly. Using LED lighting, they cut electricity for slot use 50 percent.

The Grand Traverse Band of Ottawa & Chippewa Indians demonstrate their ancient tradition of showing respect for Mother Nature is a viable way of life for modern times.

CHAPTER 7

Planet-Friendly Parks

Michigan parks are recognized and praised for their great scenic beauty and diversity. Take Sleeping Bear Dunes National Lakeshore. The park was identified as "The Most Beautiful Place in America" by ABC's *Good Morning America*. It is said that Sleeping Bear's dramatic dune formations along the Lake Michigan coast are so large and unique, they may be identified from space. Michigan's State Park System, with its 13,000 campsites, was named the top state-park system in the country by the National Recreation and Park Association. From Lake Superior's coastline to the southern border, our parks are unsurpassed. But how eco-friendly are they? The answer is—more so than a decade ago.

Parks provide residents and visitors diverse opportunities for quality outdoor recreation experiences. It is also their mission to protect and preserve Michigan's natural assets. Their management staff does so in the face of climate change, which is taking a toll on the resources. Increased air and water temperatures, a rise in water evaporation levels, shifting precipitation patterns, and stronger winds all threaten park habitats, as well as cultural and archaeological resources.

Sleeping Bear Dunes National Lakeshore and Pictured Rocks National Lakeshore participate in the National Park Service's Climate Friendly Parks program. The stewardship measure aims to mitigate climate change by reduction of greenhouse gas emissions through a comprehensive series of initiatives implemented at the park level.

Michigan State Parks forward a series of green initiatives at parks, recreation areas, and state harbors. Programs promote eco-friendly

Fig. 7. Rushing waterfalls enhance the scenery at Porcupine Mountains Wilderness State Park. Hundreds of waterfalls beautify the Leave No Trace™ "Porkies" experience. Credit: Jason Gamble.

management practices and use of eco-safe products in measures ranging from water conservation to biological control of invasive species.

Headlands International Dark Sky Park, located in Emmet County, became a world leader in addressing light pollution. One of only nine dark-sky parks on the planet, the Headlands promotes and protects opportunities for stargazers.

Michigan parks provide a diversity of experiences so many of us cherish. Whether it's chatting around the campfire, a romantic beach stroll, boating and beaching, or hiking and biking, parks enrich our lives beyond measure. Green park programs offer explorers the chance to make a difference by participating in stewardship efforts. Only in working together can we ensure the next generation is afforded the same amazing opportunities to connect to nature as we enjoy today.

Partners in Preservation

Headlands International Dark Sky Park
7725 E. Wilderness Park Drive
Mackinaw City, Michigan 49701
(231) 348-1704
www.emmetcounty.org/darkskypark

Plan to get starstruck this year. Pack a pair of binoculars and head to the tip of the Mitt to a truly stellar destination. In 2011, Emmet County's 600-acre Headlands became the sixth designated International Dark Sky Park in the United States. Situated along Lake Michigan in Emmet County, the premier stargazing park opens all new opportunities for Michigan eco-explorers.

The Dark Sky designation recognizes the value of natural darkness as a vital educational, cultural, and scenic natural resource and preserves pristine night views forever. Toss a blanket down or set up a lawn chair and simply look skyward to enjoy a heavenly show of twinkling stars, the Man in the Moon, shooting stars, and all the wonders swirling above. The International Dark-Sky Association was the first organization to focus attention on the hazards of light pollution. To achieve designation as a Dark Sky Park a public site must possess "exceptional starry skies and natural nocturnal habitat where light pollution is mitigated . . ." In 2012, Michigan legislators supported the new Emmet County resource with their approval of the Dark Sky Coast bill. The bill protects 21,000 contiguous acres surrounding the Headlands by establishing landowner rules for preserving the dark sky.

Headlands Park is located just west of Mackinaw City. Its thickly forested landscape features 5 miles of trails and 2.5 miles of shoreline. The park is free and always open. Starting from the parking area, visitors follow the 1.5-mile Headlands Dark Sky Discovery Trail to the beach for viewing. Located along the trail are 11 interpretive stations and a cell phone/smartphone audio tour. While there is no camping at the park, visitors are encouraged to stay through the night to enjoy the entire sky spectacle. The Emmet County Parks and Recreation Department regularly present family-friendly and imaginative educational events celebrating the starry dome and all it contains.

National Parks

Sleeping Bear Dunes National Lakeshore—located along Lake Michigan, and Pictured Rocks National Lakeshore—located along Lake Superior, actively participate in the National Park Service's Climate Friendly Parks program. The voluntary program promotes park measures reducing greenhouse gases and encourages visitors to adopt eco-friendly practices in daily life.

Pictured Rocks National Lakeshore
N8391 Sand Point Road
P.O. Box 40
Munising, Michigan 49862
(906) 387-3700
www.nps.gov/piro

Pictured Rocks National Lakeshore is aptly named for its multi-colored sandstone cliffs. Painted by minerals in shades of red, orange, green, tan, and white, its cliffs soar 200 feet above Lake Superior. Few outdoor experiences match the thrill of kayaking the untamed Great Lake in the shadow of the park's towering painted cliffs.

The Upper Peninsula park is located along the south shore of Lake Superior, between Munising and Grand Marais. While divided into two zones, Pictured Rocks hugs the coast for 40 miles and encompasses a total of 114 square miles. Its prized features also include the Grand Sable Dunes, six major lakes, waterfalls, 111 miles of hiking trails, three drive-in and more than a dozen hike-in camping locations, and 36 historic structures. The park provides habitat for 42 mammal species, 57 fish species, as well as fragile and protected vegetation. It's home to 15 threatened or endangered species and 12 species of concern. During winter months, a popular activity is climbing the ice sheets that form between Munising Falls and Sand Point.

Pictured Rocks is an award-winning national leader in sustainability. Park innovations include conversion of campground water pumps to a solar, chlorinated well pump system, and a solar power grid system for seasonal-employee housing. Its pioneering conversion to soy-based bio-fluids in vehicles proved the measure's viability in cold climates. In 2011, the park joined forces with the Superior Watershed Partnership and Land Trust in a community outreach program. The program inspired Alger County citizens and businesses to adopt energy-savings measures. Over 10 months, Alger Energy Savers resulted in an estimated reduction of 2,054 tons of carbon dioxide, a leading greenhouse gas contributing to climate change.

Sleeping Bear Dunes National Lakeshore
9922 Front Street
Empire, Michigan 49630
(231) 326-5134
www.nps.gov/slbe

Sleeping Bear Dunes National Lakeshore guards some of Michigan's most fragile and unique natural treasures. The park's 71,000 acres encompasses landscapes created eons ago by glacial movement. It's an exhilarating blend of immense sand dunes, 35 miles of Lake Michigan coast, inland lakes, streams, forest, meadows, bogs, seven campgrounds, two islands, 100 miles of hiking trails, a historic rural village, museums, and more.

The park stretches along the northwest coast of the Lower Peninsula in scenic Benzie and Leelanau Counties. Few places in the world can match Sleeping Bear's year-round beauty and diversity. But it, too, is under modern threats from the likes of invasive plant, animal, and insect species, increased traffic, and degradation to water and air quality.

Sleeping Bear managers developed a park plan aligned with the National Park Service's Climate Friendly Park program targeting green practices and processes. The park has accomplished significant steps toward its green goals, including replacement of oil, cleaners, and solvents with soy-based products, installation of photovoltaic systems on North and South Manitou Islands, installation of programmable thermostats, and energy-efficient lights. Other measures include building a more eco-friendly vehicle fleet and installing a visitor tire-inflation station to increase mileage and reduce greenhouse gas emissions. In 2012, the first phase of the new nonmotorized Sleeping Bear Heritage Trail opened. The paved path will extend 27 miles when completed, providing visitors additional low-impact recreation options.

Michigan State Parks

Each of Michigan's 99 state parks participates in some manner in the system's Green Initiatives program. A sustainability model for parks throughout the country, the system's key initiatives range from water conservation to biological control of nonnative species to cleaning green. Highlighted below are two parks leading the green charge.

Bay City State Recreation Area
3582 State Park Drive
Bay City, Michigan 48706
(989) 684-3020
www.michigandnr.com

Created in 1923, Bay City State Recreation Area has long been one of Michigan's most popular parks. The park sits along Lake Huron's Saginaw Bay and encompasses 2,800 acres, including the 1,800-acre Tobico Marsh wildlife refuge. Tobico Marsh is one of the largest freshwater coastal wetlands on the Great Lakes. It's a lively place with cattails swaying in the breeze and songbirds greeting the dawn. A nationally recognized birding destination, the marsh is home to more than 200 species. As many as 5,000 ducks and geese can be viewed at one time during the fall peak migration period. The 5-mile Andersen-Tobico trail showcases the wetlands, birds, deer, beaver, muskrats, mink, and otter. Two observation towers provide sweeping scenic views. Park features also include 193 electric-service campsites, 1,000 feet of sandy beach, picnic areas, and a nature center.

Bay City State Recreation Area was one of 10 state parks to adopt the original Camp Green pilot program. The pilot engaged park visitors in several stewardship initiatives. Since use of electricity is the park system's largest utility use, campers were encouraged to use RV air conditioning responsibly, to take shorter showers, to refrain from burning trash in campfires, and to use park recycling stations. The program eventually involved into a system-wide campaign aimed at raising awareness of the camper's power to make positive contributions to park sustainability.

In 2012, Bay City State Recreation Area took a bold step ending a 30-year practice. It halted chemical mosquito-control treatment. The controversial decision came out of concerns for the potential negative impact of chemical treatment on the health of campers, the people living in the vicinity, and the ecosystem. Park officials monitor mosquito counts for making future control decisions. Bay City State Recreation Area's commitment to protecting Michigan's priceless resources, at the cost of controversy, demonstrates genuine green leadership and dedication to future generations.

Porcupine Mountains Wilderness State Park
33303 Headquarters Road
Ontonagon, Michigan 49953
(906) 885-5275
www.michigandnr.com

Porcupine Mountains Wilderness State Park is situated along Lake Superior at the western edge of the Upper Peninsula in Ontonagon and Gogebic Counties. It was designated a state park in 1945 for the purpose of protecting the last large tract of Michigan's untouched hardwoods. This forest museum covers close to 94 square miles. About 35,000 acres of the ancient northern hardwood forest, one of the most prized stands in North America, is located in the heart of the park. The wilderness provides solitude and sublime attractions such as Lake of the Clouds, Summit Peak, and the Presque Isle scenic areas. There are waterfalls, 90 miles of hiking trails, 42 km of groomed cross-country ski trails, more than 150 campsites, picnic, and boating facilities, fishing, hunting, wildlife watching, and even dogsledding.

It's a lot to offer and a lot to protect. The park's green program began in mid-2000. Staff converted to near food-grade, soy-based products to run chain saws and other machinery, protecting the virgin forest from petroleum pollution. A photovoltaic system was installed to provide electricity to several buildings during the summer months. Solar is also the power source for the park's composting toilet system, a system used by as many as 200,000 people annually. Paints, green cleaners, and energy-efficient lighting are other key green conversions.

Visitors are engaged in the park's green program upon registration. It's Leave No Trace™ camping, and boot cleaners are located at trailheads to prevent introduction of nonnative plants.

The "Porkies" prove that the days of abuse, misuse, and toxic chemical use at parks can be history.

Eco Checklist for Parks

Does the park have an interpretive program focused on resource protection?
How many hybrid or alternative fuel vehicles are in the park fleet?
Does the park use soy-based oils and cleaning products?
How aggressive is the recycling program?
What alternative energy sources are used?
Are new building projects constructed with sustainable methods and materials?
How are park users involved in sustainability programs?

Beachcombing for Shipwrecks

If you ever had the itch to make your own archeological discovery, Sleeping Bear Dunes National Lakeshore is the place to visit. Beneath Lake Michigan's surface, along the 36-mile-long Manitou Passage, lie as many as 45 undiscovered historic shipwrecks doomed by storms. Fierce Great Lakes winds continue to wash ashore remnants of the long-lost wooden ships for beachcombers to make the discovery of a lifetime.

The Manitou Passage was a shortcut on the maritime highway between Chicago and Mackinaw. It was often travelled during the 1800s, the Great Lakes golden era of commercial sailing. Captains eager to beat Old Man Winter with one last cargo of the season frequently met more than they bargained for. They encountered the brutal November storms that make the lakes some of the most dangerous bodies of water on the planet. Today, Lake Michigan's notorious storms are responsible for depositing ship relics onto Sleeping Bear beaches.

These tempests unravel secrets of the past anyone may investigate. During the winter of 2012, a 50-foot ship fragment with planks five inches thick was exposed on the beach near Sleeping Bear Point and found by a hiker. In October 2010, Lake Michigan experienced one of the most violent storms in recorded history. Sixty-mph winds and 22-foot waves churned the inland sea mercilessly and beat upon her shores. For Sleeping Bear shipwreck hunters, the intense storm was fortuitous. Wreckage washed ashore during the weather event. Soon after, beachcombers came upon a relic 16 feet wide, with a 40-foot center beam. It is thought to be part of a ship that sat on the bottomland land for 150 years.

While large ship relics occasionally make shore, it's also possible for beachcombers to find small pieces of darkened, waterlogged chunks of wood or cast-iron hardware, nuts, and bolts. Small as they may be in size, it is exhilarating to stand witness to a slice of Michigan's maritime heritage.

Fall and spring, when winds of change cause high surfs, are the optimal periods for beachcombing shipwrecks. Bundle up against biting lakeshore winds. Bring your camera to record any findings, as artifacts are park property and may not be disturbed or removed.

Before heading out, stop at the park visitor center in Empire for shipwreck information and maps. One of the best places to start your exploring is the Sleeping Bear Point Life-Saving Station museum, located just west of Glen Haven. The post was built in 1901 as a rescue station for distressed ships sailing through the Manitou Passage. In its day it was the Great Lakes post known to experience the most intense winds and surf. From the museum, follow the beach toward Sleeping Bear Point. As you hike the shoreline, keep an eagle eye on the water and sand for artifacts. Photograph your finds. Park staff will later help you identify your discoveries.

Coming face to face with shipwreck relics is without question exciting. But, strolling along the Sleeping Bear shoreline in the sullen, blustery shoulder seasons has other rewards. One recognizes a beauty more subtle than summer's brilliance paints. Solitude penetrates the soul, while the cold lapping waves awaken your link to your Great Lakes heritage and the scores of brave shipmates who once sailed these waters.

CHAPTER 8

Sleep Green

Every eco-explorer needs a place to lay their head at night. Whatever your budget or personal preferences, there's a Michigan green hotel, motel, or bed and breakfast happy to tuck you in. But you might not sleep quite so peacefully once you realize that lodging is the fourth largest user of energy in the U.S. commercial sector.

The numbers demonstrate the importance of choosing green lodging. There are 47,000 hotels and motels in this country giving business and pleasure travelers a place to rest—and most of them use large amounts of energy. Guest rooms account for 6 percent of lodging's operating cost, and the industry's environmental footprint makes quite a trail. Given that most lodging facilities operate 24/7, hotels and motels create continuous resource drains. Pools, vending machines, ice makers, and intensive housekeeping practices all contribute to the problem. In addition, guests are frequently careless consumers, thoughtlessly wasting water and electricity resources.

In 2006 the Michigan Energy Office and Department of Environmental Quality Michigan decided to plug the drain. The agencies jointly launched the Green Lodging Michigan (GLM) program. In doing so, Michigan joined a growing number of states encouraging sustainability within the hospitality industry.

GLM is a voluntary, nonregulatory initiative, establishing guidelines for energy conservation, air quality, solid and toxic waste management, and reduced water consumption at hotels, motels, resorts, and bed and breakfasts. Through strategic management practices, lodgings and their guests are able to participate in conserving the state's land, air, and water resources.

Fig. 8. Powered by wind and solar, LogHaven Bed, Breakfast and Barn near West Branch offers an off-the-grid experience for guests and their horses. The B&B is surrounded by thousands of acres of forests and trails. Credit: Gail Gotter.

Program certification requires a facility to complete an assessment in which it must meet criteria in several categories. Lodgings earn one of three certification levels: Partner, Steward, or Leader, the highest category. GLM is designed to allow small mom-and-pop motels to adopt a green program, as well as Michigan's largest, newest, oldest, most remote, urban, swanky, and plain-Jane facilities to adopt a sustainable profile. Whether it's office paper or old bedsheets, the program encourages facilities to recycle, reduce, and reuse. Use of energy-efficient lighting, appliances, and heating and cooling units is emphasized. Program criteria range from the purchase of nontoxic products to eliminating hazardous materials to using refillable soap dispensers and involving guests in reusing linens and towels. Some steps lodgings embrace are simple and inexpensive; others, like installation of new, efficient heating systems, are costly. Regardless of the GLM level a lodging earns, certification identifies the establishment as a green industry leader. Guests contribute to the effort by declining housekeeping services, turning lights off when leaving rooms, taking short showers, and complying with recycling programs.

As of the writing of this book, GLM has certified 62 lodgings. Twenty-two applications were pending. The complete list can be found at www.michigan.gov/greenlodging. A quick glance at the assortment of certified establishments makes clear green lodgings come in all shapes, sizes, and across locales. The sampling of green lodgings selected for this chapter reflects this impressive diversity and the various strategies for achieving sustainability. You just might want to take the Goldilocks approach and try them all.

It is worth noting that the Green Venues Michigan program is modeled after GLM. The program was introduced in 2009 by the Michigan Department of Energy, Labor & Economic Growth and is administered by the Bureau of Energy Systems. It certifies entertainment venues, convention centers, museums, and other facilities. Like GLM, participants earn Leader, Steward, or Partner certification by adopting conservation practices. Certified venues include the Detroit Institute of Arts, Detroit's Cobo Center, DeVos Place Convention Center in Grand Rapids, Michigan International Speedway in Brooklyn, and four others. See them all at www.michigan.gov.

Green Lodging Michigan Participants

Chateau Chantal Winery and Bed & Breakfast
15900 Rue de Vin
Traverse City, Michigan 49686
(231) 223-4110
www.chateauchantal.com
GLM Partner Certification

You would be hard-pressed to find a more romantic green lodging facility anywhere in the world. Chateau Chantal is nestled on 65 acres along the scenic Old Mission Peninsula, 12 miles north of Traverse City proper. Ranked one of the top 10 wine-country inns in the United States, the Old World–style bed and breakfast enchants with vineyard and water views. There are 11 contemporary rooms to come home to after enjoying vineyard tours, wine tastings, and classes.

An early GLM program participant, Chateau Chantal's 2008 certification encompasses both the lodging and winery operation. One of its more significant commitments was the pledge to reduce operation water use by 2.5 percent. Chateau Chantal uses energy-efficient lighting, has a towel and linen reuse program, a recycling and composting program, and uses only eco-friendly cleaning products. The menu incorporates products raised onsite and foods from the region. It was a Michigan State University test site for measuring wind energy feasibility. As an agriculture business and keeper of the land, Chateau Chantal strives to move away from all chemical use.

Interlochen Motel
2275 M-137
Interlochen, Michigan 49642
(231) 276-9291
www.interlochenmotel.com
GLM Steward Certification

The Interlochen Motel demonstrates green lodging is possible at all ends of the hospitality spectrum. Owners of this 14-room motel took simple but effective measures to earn Steward certification. They added insulation, replaced all windows with energy-efficient models, replaced exterior and interior lights with compact fluorescent bulbs, replaced heating and cooling units to reduce energy use, and created a recycling program. Solar lights illuminate the landscape.

The no-frills facility is affordable and clean. Best of all is its location. It's just minutes from the world-renowned Interlochen Center for the Arts and its array of year-round concerts, plays, and cultural events. Only 10 minutes from Traverse City, the motel makes a good base from which to visit Northwest Michigan attractions, parks, waterways, and other recreational venues.

Kettunen Center
14901 4-H Drive
Tustin, Michigan 49688

(231) 829-3421
www.kettunencenter.org
GLM Partner Certification

Kettunen Center is tucked into the hills and forests of Osceola County along the shores of Center Lake. The conference and retreat facility is owned and operated by the 4-H Foundation. Located on 160 acres, 70 guest rooms provide comfortable lodging. Kettunen hosts 4-H leader training and youth programs and events supporting 4-H values, including Elderhostel and team-building programs, retreats, and conferences for state agencies, church groups, and summer camps. Activities range from kayaking to archery, to snowshoeing, to drama and crafts.

Since opening in 1961, the facility has promoted environmental stewardship. The facility effectively creates an ambiance stimulating appreciation for the wonders of nature. Green initiatives include geothermal heating and cooling, energy-efficient lighting, low-flow faucets, showerheads and fixtures, a comprehensive recycling program, and avoidance of single-use items. Program staff participates in volunteer environmental-monitoring programs including MiCorps water-quality sampling, Michigan Frog and Toad Survey, Monarch Watch, and Project Feeder Watch, an effort reporting bird activity at Kettunen feeder stations.

LogHaven Bed, Breakfast and Barn
1550 McGregor Road
West Branch, Michigan 48661
(989) 685-3527
www.loghavenbb.com
GLM Steward Certification

A wind turbine, solar panels, and a battery system meet all of LogHaven's electricity needs, allowing it to operate off the electricity grid. The appealing log B&B is situated on 80 acres surrounded by the Huron National Forest with links to recreational trails. There are three guest rooms and a barn to bed horses for those planning equestrian treks. The B&B's conservation measures include low-flow fixtures and energy-efficient appliances. Operators avoid single-serve and single-use items. LogHaven promotes energy conservation with monthly seminars conducted onsite. Programs introduce home and business owners to the basics of alternative energy.

Peaches Bed and Breakfast
29 Gay Avenue SE
Grand Rapids, Michigan 49503
(616) 454-8000
www.peaches-inn.com
GLM Leader Certification

In 2011, Peaches Bed and Breakfast in Grand Rapids became the first Michigan lodging to provide guests an overnight electric vehicle charging station. The gracious Georgian manor houses five spacious guest rooms, a library, and game room. Located within walking distance of Grand Rapid's popular downtown venues, this classy, one-of-a-kind B&B truly stands out in the sustainable lodging movement.

Peaches green initiatives include recycling 90 percent of waste generated at the inn, elimination of disposable products, and conversion to energy-efficient appliances. Operators dry sheets in the fresh air and purchase supplies locally. A kitchen garden located on the rooftop provides food for gourmet breakfasts while serving to help control interior temperatures. It is the innkeeper's policy to continually seek eco-safe products and services for an ever-greener lodging experience.

Royal Park Hotel
600 East University Drive
Rochester, Michigan 48307
(248) 652-2600
www.royalparkhotel.net
GLM Steward Certification

If you prefer the royal treatment, you'll like this eco-conscious luxury boutique hotel located in the metro Detroit area. The four-star Royal Park Hotel offers Old World charisma to travelers from around the globe. Its 143 rooms, guest library and business center, and dining options provide all the amenities one would expect from a world-class lodging. The location affords easy access to southeast Michigan's finest shopping, museums, and entertainment venues, as well as hospitals, universities, and business hubs.

Royal Park's green program embodies basic conservation practices such as energy-efficient lighting, recycling, low-flow fixtures, and guest towel-reuse initiatives. It offers paperless check-in and check-out and provides newspapers only upon request to reduce paper consumption. Guest toiletries are 100 percent natural or certified organic with minimal packaging. A reformulation of water levels and temperatures in the laundry process resulted in saving 455,098 gallons of water annually. Its culinary team promotes sustainable practices by incorporating locally grown organic produce into the menus. Fryer grease is recycled. Produce trimmings are transported to local farms to feed livestock, closing the farm-to-table circle.

Stafford's Perry Hotel
100 Lewis Street
Petoskey, Michigan 49770
(800) 737-1899
www.staffords.co/perry-hotel-4/
GLM Leader Certified

In 2007, Stafford's Perry Hotel became the first facility to earn Green Lodging Michigan Leader certification. This historic Petoskey hotel is listed on the National Register of Historic Places and is a registered Michigan Historic Site. Built in 1899, when Great Lakes steamers brought tourists to Little Traverse Bay, the hotel remains a testament to the elegance of the period. The Perry is situated in downtown Petoskey, overlooking the gorgeous bay waters. There are 79 guest rooms, indoor dining, a rose garden for open-air dining, and a pub. Beaching, shopping, galleries, and a museum are all within walking distance.

Green initiatives include installation of high-efficiency boilers and water heaters. The system is 93 percent efficient in heating guest rooms and domestic water. The hotel has a comprehensive recycling program and low-flow faucets, showerheads, and fixtures. It also takes a green leadership role through employee training on environmental issues and public initiatives, raising public awareness of the facility's eco-friendly measures.

The Listening Inn
339 Clark Road
Crystal Falls, Michigan 49920
(906) 822-7738
www.thelisteninginn.com
GLM Leader Certification

A wilderness escape located in the far western Upper Peninsula, The Listening Inn captures the rugged sense of adventure and self-reliance characterizing the region. The 10,000-square-foot lodge was hand built by its owners from red pines harvested on the property. A mammoth stone fireplace and cedar furniture establish the back-to-nature feel. The B&B's six guest rooms feature giant log beds fit for Paul Bunyan. There are 14 km of groomed cross-country trails and separate snowshoe trails for winter fun.

The Listening Inn's sustainability measures include wood heating, a linen- and towel-reuse program, a comprehensive recycling program, and energy-efficient lighting. Its 520 acres are enrolled in a forest management program. Most fruits and vegetables served to guests are grown onsite. As a bonus to all the Upper Peninsula amenities, guests may purchase maple syrup produced on the property and the inn's homemade jams.

The Westin Detroit Metropolitan Airport
2501 Worldgateway Place
Detroit, Michigan 48242
(734) 942-6500
www.westindetroitmetroairport.com
GLM Steward Certification

The Westin Detroit Metropolitan Airport offers convenience in a green package. Located in the airport, it provides guests a private security entrance to the Edward H. McNamara Terminal. The Westin is the only upscale hotel in the airport. It offers 24-hour shuttle service to the north terminal, 404 guest rooms, 10 suites, 28 meeting rooms, a fitness studio, and indoor pool.

The Westin's green practices include high-efficiency lighting, water conserving fixtures, alternatives to bottled water, and recycling. The hotel eliminated Styrofoam packaging. Sustainable food and beverage options are made available. Practices also include green housekeeping, integrated pest management, and use of low-emitting paints, floorings, and furniture. Guests may participate in Westin's Green Choice program to earn rewards by declining housekeeping services. For every night housekeeping is declined, guests conserve on average 49.2 gallons of water, enough electricity to run a laptop for 10 hours, and prevent adding 7 ounces of chemicals into the environment.

Eco Checklist for Lodging

Has the facility installed low-flow fixtures for water conservation?

Are guests able to decline housekeeping services?

Is there an extensive recycling program?

Has the facility installed energy-efficient heating/cooling units and appliances?

Are refillable dispensers used for toiletries to reduce packaging waste?

Is there electronic check-in and check-out?

Does the kitchen incorporate local foods in the menu?

The Audacious CityFlats

When CityFlatsHotel opened in 2008, it made an audacious statement to the hospitality industry by demonstrating it is possible for a modern hotel to be chic, appealing, comfortable—and green. The five-story hotel in downtown Holland, opened by the Holland-based Charter House Innovations, was the Midwest's first LEED Gold Certified hotel.

This 56-room facility set sustainability standards others in the industry still strive to match. A sleek European styling is evident throughout the green hotel. Floor-to-ceiling windows and 10–13-foot ceilings maximize natural lighting. The effect is an expansive, elegant ambiance. But the hotel's true beauty is in its thoughtful, environmentally sound construction.

Some of CityFlats' eco-friendly features are cork flooring installed with low-VOC adhesives, low-flow faucets and toilets, countertops made from Cradle-to-Cradle Certified recycled glass and concrete, low-VOC paint, and high-efficiency heating and cooling units with occupancy sensors.

No two rooms are alike at this trendsetting hotel. Its furniture is sustainable and manufactured locally, including the popular CityDrem mattresses topping platform beds covered by bamboo linens. The eco-statement is repeated down to bath products, the organic fair-trade coffee served, and local foods incorporated into its restaurant menus. Electric car charging stations are found in the hotel parking lot.

In 2010, Charter House Innovations opened a second hotel in downtown Grand Rapids. The boutique green facility revived the historic Fox Jeweler Building, constructed in 1875. Also designed for LEED Gold Certification, the 28-room Grand Rapids location was built with more than 30 percent of materials acquired from local sources, and includes seating and décor manufactured in Holland.

Governor Rick Snyder personally presented hotel representatives with the 2012 Good Earth Keeping Award. The honor recognizes lodging properties that successfully integrate sound environmental practices into daily operations and that deliver quality service.

CityFlats hotels allow you to enjoy a fully sustainable urban experience. The hotels place you in the thick of the action in both the highly walkable Holland, with its delightful shops, pubs, theaters, and eateries, and Grand Rapids. In Grand Rapids, CityFlatsHotel guests are within walking distance of the Grand Rapids Art Museum, the world's first newly built LEED-certified museum, and the DeVos Place Convention Center, one of a handful of certified Michigan Green Venues. The ability to get around by foot and bicycle allows visitors to see the sights without relying on fossil-fuel energy. The American Bicycle Association ranked the city in the top 50 bicycle-friendly cities in America.

From the roof over your head to the pillow you sleep upon, to your exploration of two of Michigan's most engaging cities, the green city experience is an uplifting exploration into sustainability.

CityFlatsHotel-Holland
61 East 7th St.
Holland, Michigan 49423
(616) 796-2100

CityFlatsHotel-Grand Rapids
83 Monroe Center St. NW
Grand Rapids, Michigan 49503
(616) 608-1720
http://www.cityflatshotel.com

CHAPTER 9

Tread Softly

It's amazing the places two feet will take a Michigan eco-explorer. A pair of shoes and you're good to climb to the top of mountains, wander wilderness and hike to monuments of Michigan's heritage.

The state's vast trail network offers a multitude of first-rate possibilities for low-impact outdoor recreation. With 2,300 miles of trails to trek, Michigan's rails-to-trails system ranks number one in the nation. Michigan's expanding trail system welcomes an increase in the popularity of biking. Industry experts believe the state is on the verge of becoming one of America's leading bicycling destinations. Eight Michigan communities are already ranked bicycle friendly by the League of American Bicyclists: Ann Arbor, Grand Rapids, Houghton, Lansing, Marquette, Midland, Portage, Traverse City, and Marquette. Federal, state, county, township, city, and private investment supports new trail connections throughout the Mitten State. This medley of pathways affords nearly everyone easy access to a diversity of earth-friendly adventures.

Individual trails range from short paths meandering through neighborhood parks to those spanning unspoiled backcountry for nearly 200 miles. The 2,700-mile-long North Country Trail weaves for 1,150 miles through the Lower and Upper Peninsulas, linking Michigan to the trail system in six states. Michigan trails encircle pristine waters, crown massive dunes, and hug wetlands. Trails accommodate hiking and biking activities, cross-country skiing, snowshoeing, and dogsledding. Some provide universal access for the physically challenged, with boardwalks friendly to wheelchairs and even strollers. Regardless of our abilities or backgrounds, outdoor trails bring us closer to nature. But from nature's perspective, this may be too much of a good thing.

Sleeping Bear Dunes National Lakeshore provides a case in point. The park historically welcomed 1.2 million visitors annually. The year after ABC's *Good Morning America* recognized the park as 2011's "America's Most Beautiful Place," attendance jumped roughly 30 percent. That adds up to a lot of feet trekking park trails along fragile dunes, beaches, and backcountry.

In light of the popularity of Michigan's natural places, preservation is a critical matter. The privilege of rubbing elbows with flora and fauna calls for us to enjoy the outdoors responsibly in order that we may protect the integrity of Michigan's natural places. The cumulative environmental footprint resulting from increased numbers of trail users places the burden of preservation on each individual explorer. One of the most important practices responsible trail users employ is a commitment to remaining on trails. Two feet or two wheels may not leave a significant impact on the environment, but hundreds, thousands, even millions, are sure to follow.

National parks, several Michigan state parks, nature centers, campgrounds, and municipal parks and recreation departments advocate Leave No Trace™ practices. These guidelines set forth by the Center for Outdoor Ethics for public lands are bound within seven points. Topic areas address trip preparation, surface impact, waste disposal, use of fire, consideration for wildlife and people, and the importance of leaving behind any finds. If you're not familiar with Leave No Trace™ guidelines, visit http://Int.org/learn/7-principles for comprehensive suggestions for leaving the wilds undisturbed. At participating parks, rangers are able to advise visitors on these practices and provide information regarding any especially sensitive natural features within the park or preserve.

The state's trail system beckons us to the wilds, but trails also exist for the purpose of leading us to a greater knowledge of who we are as Michiganders. Cultural trails highlight state history, architecture, and social milestones, allowing us to walk and wheel our way to our past, present and future. Trails empower us to uncover secrets of man, beast, and elements. It's exhilarating, fun, and there's likely a trail not far from your own front door.

Michigan's Final Frontiers

Greenstone Ridge Trail
Isle Royale National Park
800 East Lakeshore Drive
Houghton, Michigan 49931
(906) 482-0984
www.nps.gov/isro

Lake Superior's largest island, Congress established Isle Royale as a wilderness preserve in 1931. President Franklin Roosevelt designated it a national park in 1940. Isle Royale consists of the main island and a chain of 450 small islands. The park preserves 850 square miles, including submerged land. It is accessed only by boat or sea plane, which limits visitors to the most devoted explorers.

Ninety-eight percent of the island is designated wilderness. While Isle Royale features 165 miles of trails, its Greenstone Ridge Trail is on every serious Midwest backpacker's bucket list. Greenstone is named for the Isle Royale greenstone, designated as the official state gem in 1973.

The trail stretches across the heart of the island for 42.5 miles, from Lookout Louise on the eastern end to the Windigo visitor's center at the island's western tip. The trail tests your survival skills while rewarding you with moments of peace, silence, and wonder. Mostly wooded, Greenstone Ridge Trail is defined by solitude, views spanning 50 miles, and the possibility for encounters with moose, wolves, and fox. Peak elevations reach 1,300-plus feet with overlooks offering breathtaking vistas. Greenstone Ridge is rated as requiring moderate hiking ability levels, although it may be suitable for some beginners. Considered the region's premier distance hike, the trail requires four to five days for most hikers to complete. Six camping sites dot the wilderness pathway. The park is open April through October.

Trap Hills
Ottawa National Forest
Supervisor's Office

Fig. 9. A hiker treks the North Country Trail near Mesick. Michigan's segment of the seven-state trail system features 1,150 miles of pathway weaving across both peninsulas. Credit: Sally Barber.

E6248 US 2
Ironwood, Michigan 49938
(906) 932-1330
http://www.fs.usda.gov/recarea/ottawa/recreation/hiking/
    recarea/?recid=12328&actid=51

Trap Hills showcases the rugged splendor of the Upper Midwest. This ridge line is located in the Upper Peninsula's Ontonagon County, deep within the Ottawa National Forest. Hikers are rewarded with sublime panoramic views and a lively array of wildlife hooting and howling in the night. There are rocky perches for pondering life's mysteries, crystal-clear streams, and rare plants such as Fairy Bells and Braun's Holly Fern. Two hundred acres of old growth forest lie within the area.

A section of the North Country Trail runs through Trap Hills. The trailhead is found along Old M-64, two miles north of Bergman. It rises and falls through the ridges for 34 miles to Old Victoria, a restored mining community. Sights along the trail include four waterfalls, stream gorges, and mining artifacts dating back to the nineteenth-century heyday. A number of day hikes are mapped by the North Country Trail Association. They encompass distances as short as a half-mile. Download maps at www.northcountrytrail.or/pwf/traphills.htm. These trails are suitable for most hikers. The Trap Hills area is open year-round. Winter hikers are advised to prepare for difficult conditions.

Trekking Diversity

Access Adventure Trail
Chipp-A-Waters Park
1403 West High Street
Mount Pleasant, Michigan 48858
(989) 799-5335
www.mt-pleasant.org

Everyone deserves the opportunity to explore. That's why the city of Mount Pleasant developed the Access Adventure Trail, a universally accessible pathway through the community's most scenic areas. The trail begins at the 30-acre Chipp-A-Waters Park, located on the city's west side, and connects to the barrier-free, three-mile Riverwalk Pathway. The riverwalk follows the Chippewa River through five parks and into the downtown district. A specially designed eight-foot-wide bridge across the river allows wheelchair users an unobstructed view of the scenery. Other trail features are turnouts with fixed scopes positioned at wheelchair level for spotting wildlife, accessible tables, benches, and interpretive signs.

Pointe Mouillee State Game Area
Pointe Mouillee DNR Field Office
37205 Mouillee Road
Rockwood, Michigan 48173
(734) 379-9692
www.michigandnr.com

Dikes create an uncommon trail system through a distinctive preserve, the Pointe Mouillee State Game Area. Straddling Monroe and Wayne Counties, Pointe Mouillee State Game Area is the result of the world's largest freshwater marsh restoration project. The 4,000-acre reserve is located near Rockwood, at the mouth of the Huron River at Lake Erie. In 1945, the state acquired a portion of this acreage from a private sportsman's club and later purchased additional surrounding property. After the barrier island washed out, the Army Corps of Engineers built a new one from materials dredged from harbors and shipping channels. A Confined Disposal Facility was built on 700 acres to contain these polluted materials. Dikes were constructed around the facility to serve as a barrier for the marsh. Today, these manmade structures provide opportunities for eco-explorers.

The wetland dike system provides one of Michigan's most unique opportunities for mountain biking, hiking, and wildlife watching. Routes range from 2 to 10 miles. The dikes provide a truly up close and personal experience with the preserve's wildlife family.

With about 300 bird species spotted at Point Mouillee, it is one of Michigan's top birding sites. Waterfowl, shorebirds, wading birds, and birds of prey offer exceptional bird-watching opportunities in late summer and early fall. Both common and rare birds are found here, including loons, herons, the American white pelican, Snow Goose, trumpeter and tundra swan, pheasants, cormorants, partridges, gulls, terns, and others. For more than 60 autumns, the preserve has hosted the Pointe Mouillee Waterfowl Festival. Highlights include goose- and duck-calling championships.

Loda Lake Wildflower Sanctuary
Baldwin/White Cloud Ranger District
U.S. Forest Service
4794 6 Mile Road
White Cloud, Michigan 47946
(231) 745-4631
http://www.fs.fed.us/wildflowers/regions/eastern/LodaLake/index
    .shtml

Loda Lake National Wildflower Sanctuary in Newaygo County is the only wildflower sanctuary within the national forest system. The 72-acre preserve dates back to the late 1930s, when the Michigan Garden Club agreed to partner with the government in managing the sanctuary. Located within the Manistee National Forest, the preserve features a spring-fed lake, marsh, and woodlands containing more than 230 plant species. Spring is the most popular season to visit the sanctuary, as wildflowers begin to add a colorful burst to the landscape. A self-guided tour follows the 1.5-mile trail marked by 42 interpretive posts coordinated with a descriptive brochure available at the trailhead.

Wildflowers viewed at Loda Lake include pink lady's slipper, jack-in-the-pulpit, wild columbine, swamp milkweed, and round-leaved sundew. A bee-pollinator garden was established at the sanctuary in 2008. The nonmotorized trail is rated moderately easy. You'll find a bench along the way to rest or to simply sit and soak in the beauty. It's a nice day outing, as picnic facilities are available, as well as a launch for canoes and kayaks.

Sinkholes Pathway
Mackinaw State Forest
M-33 and Tomahawk Lake Highway
Onaway, Michigan 49765
(989) 785-4251
http://www.michigandnr.com/parksandtrails/details
    .aspx?id=52&type=SFPW

Sinkholes Pathway, located near Onaway, is one of Michigan's most unusual trails. The 2.5-mile pathway is accessed from Shoepac Lake State Forest Campground. The trail encompasses five sinkholes. A viewing platform near the trailhead provides a bird's-eye view of this geological wonder. A 180-step stairway leads 100 feet down to the sinkhole's bottom. A short loop makes sinkhole viewing possible for those with less stamina or time. Sinkholes Pathway connects to the 80-mile High Country Pathway traversing Presque Isle, Cheboygan, Otsego, and Montmorency Counties. Hiking, biking, and camping are easily incorporated into day visits or multiday excursions.

Presque Isle and Alpena Counties are sinkhole central in Michigan. More than 200 sinkholes are found here, including sinkholes at Lake Huron's bottom in Thunder Bay. This entire northeastern Michigan area, known as the karst region, features limestone bedrock prone to erosion from subterranean streams. Weakened areas eventually collapse into conical caverns, or sinkholes.

While most Michigan sinkholes are located on private property, Stevens Twin Sinks Preserve in Alpena County provides another viewing option. Located five miles south of Posen along Leer Road, the preserve features two sinkholes, each 200 feet in diameter and 85 feet deep.

Winter Wanderlust

Despite the fact Michigan features 3,000 miles of cross-country ski trails, there's room for conflict among users. Nonmotorized, multiuse trails are designated for winter use by cross-country skiers, snowshoers, and dogsledders, but shared use often diminishes quality experiences. Trails groomed for cross-country skiing are spoiled by snowshoe traffic and dog paws, while groomed trails rob snowshoers of the pleasure of blazing through a fresh snowfall. At the same time, going off-trail with snowshoes risks ecosystem damage. Mushing trails require openings of up to eight feet to accommodate passing sleds, wider than needed by snowshoers. To live in harmony is possible when trails are selected for dedicated use. However, few dedicated trails currently exist outside of resort properties. Until more are developed, responsible trail users will extend respect to accommodate fellow users.

Corsair Trails
Huron-Manistee National Forest
Huron Shores Ranger Station
5671 North Skeels Avenue
Oscoda, Michigan 48750
(989) 739-0728

Cross-country skiing on the state's sunrise side provides one of the

Midwest's finest trail experiences. Since the 1930s, skiers have prized opportunities afforded by the Corsair Trails, located near Tawas. The well-designed, well-marked trails system is one of the largest groomed networks in Michigan. Corsair beckons with 28.3 miles of groomed paths rolling through the beautiful Silver Valley. Surrounded by 120,000-acre Huron National Forest, trails traverse open landscapes, northern woodlands, hills and bowls, and rustic bridges. Overall length of the premier trail system is 44.5 miles.

Three distinct sections offer options for the novice and experienced skier. The Corsair Trailhead provides a moderate challenge. Features include a 600-foot interpretive trail along Silver Creek. The Silver Valley Trailhead is defined by gentle terrain, while Wright's Lake Trailhead leads to longer loops and steeper hill country.

Skiing trails are open 24/7 beginning November 1, when snowfall permits. A warming shelter welcomes skiers on weekends.

Fort Custer Recreation Area
5163 Fort Custer Drive
Augusta, Michigan 49012
(269) 731-4200
www.michigandnr.com

Sleepy Hollow State Park
7835 East Price Road
Laingsburg, Michigan 48848
(517) 651-6217
www.michigandnr.com

Dog-powered fun is on tap year-round at Fort Custer Recreation Area and Sleepy Hollow State Park. Both facilities open trails for winter dogsledding, and summer dog team training. Sleepy Hollow is located 15 miles northeast of Lansing. The park encompasses 2,600 acres. Features include a riverway, woods, fields, and Lake Ovid nestled into the center of the park. Of the 16 miles of trails, 6.5 miles are open to dogsledding.

Located between Battle Creek and Kalamazoo, Fort Custer State

Recreation Area sits on 3,033 acres. The property was originally farm-land, converted to a U.S. Army training center during World War II and designated Michigan parkland in 1971. Twenty-five miles of multi-use trails meander through open brush, and second-growth forest. The park's ungroomed multiuse trails are open to dogsledding, but sections are marked specifically for mushers. In the past, Fort Custer hosted the annual Mid-Union Sled Haulers dogsled races. Lack of snow in recent years canceled the event; however, mushers continue to gather each winter to celebrate the sport.

Baraga State Park
1300 US-41 South
Baraga, Michigan 49908
(906) 353-6558
www.michigandnr.com

Michigan state parks, nature centers, state forests, national forests, and local parks provide trail systems compatible for snowshoe adven-tures. A six-inch snow base is generally required for good snowshoe trekking. While snowshoeing is gaining popularity as a winter pastime, it was once a necessary mode of transportation. Just off Highway 41, between L'Anse and Baraga, stands the six-story Shrine of the Snowshoe Priest, overlooking Lake Superior's Keweenaw Bay. The bronze figure of the beloved priest, and later bishop, Frederic Baraga floats in clouds holding a pair of 28-foot snowshoes. In the 1830s, Baraga traversed the Upper Peninsula, ministering to the Native American population. He traveled as many as 700 miles each winter on snowshoe to care for his flock. Baraga County, the city, and Baraga State Park honor the Snow-shoe Priest with his name.

Today, the Upper Peninsula is known as a prime area for recreational snowshoeing. Baraga State Park is located almost in the shadows of Fa-ther Baraga's statue. It's a tiny, 58-acre gem sitting along Keweenaw Bay and tucked into hardwoods. While the park's nature trail is less than one mile long, it's a peaceful spot to snowshoe and take in the subtle beauty of the frozen scenery.

Along the Cultural Trail

Foot and biking tours provide diverse low-impact opportunities to explore Michigan culture. Cities across the state offer self-guided walking tours. Ludington's Mural Walls Tour through its downtown district features 12 building murals tracing the community's history. The Petoskey walking tour showcases the city's historic buildings and stops at some of writer Ernest Hemingway's favorite youthful haunts. The Grand Rapids foot trail encompasses world history. See dinosaur bones, a piece of the Berlin Wall, the Gerald Ford Presidential Museum, a tribute to civil rights activist Rosa Parks, and more. Check with any city's visitor bureau for available self-guided tour maps.

Purple Gang Walking Tour
309 North Superior Street
Albion, Michigan 49224
(517) 629-5510
www.albiondda.org

If you like crime stories, the Albion Purple Gang Walking Tour was made for you. Promoted by the city's downtown development authority, this self-guided tour exposes secrets of some of Michigan's most notorious criminals, the Purple Gang. The Purple Gang ruled Detroit's underworld during the Prohibition era. It is believed the gang was responsible for as many as 500 murders. When Prohibition ended, remaining gang members relocated operations to Albion. The central location provided easy access to organized-crime activities in both Detroit and Chicago.

Albion's one-hour walking tour features eight Purple Gang sites, including the alley where they roughed-up enemies, the theater balcony where they met to discuss "business," the building where they stored their crime mobile, a sedan with revolving license plates and removable seats allowing for transport of stolen safes. Other highlights include the jail where members once served time and a grocery store the gang robbed. Purple Gang tour maps are available at www.albion.dda.

Michigan Legacy Art Park
12500 Crystal Mountain Drive
Thompsonville, Michigan 49683
(231) 378-4963
www.michlegacyartpark.org

The 1.6-mile Michigan Legacy Art Park trail through the hilly forests of Benzie County is dotted with 45 major works of art and 30 poetry stones celebrating the spirit and heritage of the Mitten State. The sculpture collection links hikers to the people, milestones, and natural resources forging Michigan's legacy, telling our story beneath a canopy of trees. Founded by the internationally renowned Michigan sculptor David Barr in 1995, the art trail operates as a nonprofit in cooperation with Crystal Mountain Resort. The park's 30-acre preserve is leased from the resort for a token $1 each year.

Works in the collection include several of Barr's pieces and sculptures by Michigan favorites such as Dewey Blocksma and Patricia Innis. One section is devoted to student works. The large outdoor pieces are placed in harmony with natural surroundings to inspire curiosity and compel discovery. An amphitheater situated along the trail is the site of summer concerts filling the woods with song. The sculpture park is a joyful experience and offers a unique opportunity for winter snowshoe hikes. Expect a small admission fee.

Underground Railroad Bicycle Route
Detroit Alternate Route
Adventure Cycling Association
(406) 721-1776
www.adventurecycling.org

The Underground Railroad Bicycle Route allows you to retrace the clandestine journey of slaves escaping to Michigan along a network of secret paths and safe houses in the mid-1800s. The Ohio-Detroit-Windsor cycling route developed by the Adventure Cycling Association was introduced in 2012 as part of a 2,000-mile freedom route stretching from Mobile Bay, Alabama, to Lake Huron's Georgian Bay. The 518-mile Detroit Alternate route was developed with support from the National Park Service, the City of Detroit Historic Commission, the Greenway Alliance, and the University of Pittsburg Center for Minority Health.

Beginning from Oberlin, Ohio, cyclists travel the corridor visiting former safe houses, museums, monuments, and other significant points related to slavery. The route follows western Lake Erie and crosses into Canada north of Detroit. Michigan highlights include more than 30 historical points in Blissfield, Adrian, Albion, Marshall, Saline, Ann Arbor, Ypsilanti, Romulus, and Detroit. Detroit features include Greektown's Second Baptist Church, the site of a pivotal meeting between John Brown and Frederick Douglass. Also on the map are the Elmwood cemetery—the burial grounds of several abolitionists, and the Charles H. Wright Museum of African American History—the world's largest museum dedicated to the African American quest for freedom. The route takes advantage of Detroit bike lanes, expected to total 155 miles by 2014. Underground Railroad Bike Route maps may be purchased at www.adventurecycling.org.

Detroit's effort to develop a bike-friendly city encourages low-impact discovery and group rides. These have included Art Ride, Jewish History Tour Ride, and a U.S. Social Forums ride.

Eco Checklist for Trails

Stay on the trail or designated pathway.
Use chemical-free mosquito repellant and biodegradable products.
Protect the water source by limiting activities within 200 feet of
    shorelines.
Use a portable cook stove rather than campfire.
Take out waste.
Respect the wildlife.

High-Mileage Snowshoes

It was mostly by chance that Steve Herkner and Scott Griner wound up in the snowshoe business. The convenience-store owner and towing-company operator stumbled upon a good eco thing—and it changed their lives.

Several years ago, serendipity provided the men a couple pairs of handmade snowshoes from a worker employed at a Grand Traverse County tire-recycling facility. The snowshoes were crudely constructed from scrap tires, but they worked great for tromping through late winter snows in Griner's sugarbush, another of his enterprises. The 40-acre maple-syrup operation required much trekking to install taps and gather sap. Eventually, the men wanted to replace the snowshoes.

They returned to the inventor, who had no interest in building more snowshoes. So, in the late 2000s, Herkner and Griner bought rights to the concept and the two entrepreneurs developed their own process for building snowshoes from scrap tires. S&S Snowshoes was born.

The entrepreneurs retained the best features from the original snowshoes. Especially important was the flexibility provided by tire material. They improved upon small details. To the hand-cut tire material, they incorporated high-strength cloth straps and industrial-grade washers and rivets. The end product is a lightweight, durable, and easy to use snowshoe they call Treadrite Snowshoes.

Each snowshoe continues to be hand built at the men's small manufacturing facility in Benzie County. Tires for the snowshoes are obtained from a recycling facility near Clare. Only tire sides are used in constructing Treadrites. Tread sections of the tires are returned to the recycler, where they are shredded for use as mulch or other purposes. Each pair of snowshoes requires about two hours to craft. Treadrites are constructed in four sizes determined by tire widths.

Unlike today's mass-manufactured snowshoes, which are designed primarily for use on groomed trails, Treadrite snowshoes perform well in deep, pristine snow. They give when walking over downed branches or other obstacles, and allow for tight turns. Not only has the snowshoe's performance been proven in the northern sugarbush and trails, they've been praised by users from the Pacific Northwest to the swamplands of Florida.

Herkner and Griner plan to keep their snowshoe business small, for now. Only about 200 pair are produced annually. If you can't get to Herkner's Pantry Shelf store located outside of Traverse City to purchase a pair, Treadrites can be ordered online at www.sssnowshoes.com. It's an opportunity for snowshoers to take the reuse, recycle mantra straight to Michigan's great outdoors and support a sustainable local economy in the process.

Epilogue

What Now?

Now that you are a Michigan eco-explorer, go forward. If we each take a baby step or two, we'll build momentum for preserving our natural world for those to come.

You may want to begin by showing appreciation for what is already accomplished. If you've enjoyed a great eco-friendly experience, recognize the efforts of the resort or park with an email, or post a positive comment on their website. While you're at it, share suggestions for future green improvements.

Take a different direction in your buying habits. Investigate ways you can personally green your favorite activity. If you're in the market for equipment, consider buying used. If you prefer new equipment, you'll find all types of outdoor gear now made from recycled plastics, and new bio-plastics are quickly proving a practical material for use in manufacturing. Kayaks made from recycled plastic and bamboo downhill skis and boards are good green alternative choices. Tents, sleeping bags, and backpacks made from recycled materials are also readily available. Outdoor clothing manufactured from hemp, cotton, or bamboo is comfortable and attractive. Tread lightly in hiking boots made from recycled materials. Even biodegradable shoes have hit the market. Look for ways to reduce chemical use. Natural sunscreens and insect repellants are good for you and better for nature. One small step at a time can take us far.

Getting a child onboard your next adventure is a sure way to build a lasting corps for resource protection. Our opportunities to travel and explore new places and activities are unprecedented in human history. Generations to come deserve the same privilege. Consider taking a child on your next eco-adventure. It could be a relative, a friend's child, your child's friend, or a neighbor. Immersion in outdoor activities is critical in establishing a child's lifelong love affair with the things of nature. But such opportunities for the twenty-first-century child are sadly vanishing. In his book, *Last Child in the Woods,* Richard Louv writes: "For a new generation, nature is more abstraction than reality. Increasingly, nature is something to watch, to consume, to wear—to ignore." Louv stresses the importance of nature experiences for a child's healthy physical and emotional growth. It's also a vital step for ensuring the will and strength of natural resource conservation continues.

Adventure well but think local. Expand your commitment to greening your home, your office, schools, and community. Take small steps. Get that home energy audit you've put off. Carpool the kids to school, even if it's a bit less convenient. Ask your employer to switch to nontoxic housekeeping products. Volunteer for a bird survey monitoring your feeder. We can ensure sustainability and inspire others to do the same. It starts with each of us committing to taking just one small step.

BIBLIOGRAPHY

Introduction

Greenpeace. "Greenwashing." http://stopgreenwash.org/. Accessed December 15, 2012.

International Ecotourism Society, The. http://www.ecotourism.org/. Accessed December 15, 2012.

"Michigan Conservation Summary." LandScope America. http://www.land scope.org/michigan/overview. Accessed December 8, 2012.

Michigan Economic Development Corporation. May 2010. "Michigan Travel Economic Impact and Travel Volumes." http://ref.michigan.org/cm/attach /7FCE50AA-1D21-411D-A4CE-B2C55EE09612/2009_Travelresearch.pdf. Accessed December 17, 2012.

Thompson, Carol. "How to Purchase a Carbon Offset You Can Trust." July, 23, 2010. http://www.thedailygreen.com/environmental-news/latest/carbon-offset -guide. Accessed December 17, 2012.

"What is Sustainable Tourism?" Institute for Tourism. http://www.iztzg.hr/en /odrzivi_razvoj/sustainable_tourism/. Accessed December 28, 2012.

Chapter 1

Envirosurfer. "The Toxicity of Surfing." InMotion Kitesurfing. http://www.in motionkitesurfing.com/2011/surfing-infographic. Accessed December 28, 2012.

"Fact Sheet 9." Clearwater News & Bulletins. http://www.clearwater.org/news/ twostrokes.html. Accessed December 20, 2012.

"Ice Sailing in Pure Michigan." Interview with Dan Hill, Pure Michigan Connect, February 15, 2012. http://www.michigan.org/blog/events/ice-sailing-in-pure-michigan/. Accessed December 28, 2012.

"On the Water." Fragile Handle With Care. http://www.dnr.state.md.us/bay /protect/water.html. Accessed December 15, 2012.

"Thunder Bay Marine Sanctuary." National Marine Sanctuaries National Oceanic & Atmospheric Administration. http://thunderbay.noaa.gov/. Accessed September 10, 2012.

Zacharias, Pat. "Sailing on Lake St. Clair's Icy Winter Winds." *Detroit News*, February 8, 1998. http://apps.detnews.com/apps/history/index.php?id=141. Accessed December 29, 2012.

Chapter 2

Blevins, Jason. "Makers of Lifts Finally Catering to Smaller Ski Areas." *Denver Post*, March 4, 2011. http://www.denverpost.com/business/ci_17535471. Accessed November 5, 2012.

"Economic Impacts of Climate Change on Michigan." Center for Integrative Research, University of Maryland, July 2008. http://www.cier.umd .edu/climateadaptation/Michigan%20Economic%20Impacts%20of%20 Climate%20Change.pdf. Accessed October 18, 2012.

Hargrove, Kelli. "Father of Snowboard Honored with Snurfer Sculpture." Transworld Business, June 6, 2012. http://business.transworld.net/99683/news /father-of-snowboarding-honored-with-snurfer-sculpture/. Accessed December 22, 2012.

"National Ski Association Organized in Ishpeming." Michigan State University Red Tape Blog, February 21, 1904. http://blogpublic.lib.msu.edu/index.php /february-21-1904-national-ski?blog=5. Accessed December 22, 2012.

SMI Snow Makers. www.snowmakers.com. Accessed November 14, 2012.

"Snow Making & Grooming at Nub's Nob." Nub's Nob. http://www.nubsnob .com/index.php?option=com_content&view=article&id=91&Itemid=123. Accessed November 18, 2012.

"Sustainable Slopes Annual Report 2010." National Ski Association. http:// www.nsaa.org/media/20935/ssar-10.pdf. Accessed October 10, 2012.

"What's New on Michigan's Ski Slopes for the Winter of 2012/2013." Michigan Ski Association. http://www.nsaa.org/media/20935/ssar-10.pdf. Accessed December 5, 2012.

Chapter 3

"Black River Watershed Management Plan." Michigan Department of Environmental Quality. Last modified September 2009. http://www.michigan

.gov/documents/deq/wb-nps-Black-River-wmp1_303607_7.pdf. Accessed October 12, 2012.

Campbell, Aaron. "Stand Up Paddleboarding in Michigan." SUP Connect. http://supconnect.mylocallineup.com/SUP-Destinations/stand-up-paddle-board-in-michigan.html. Accessed December 28, 2012.

"Carbon Footprints Factsheet." University of Michigan Center for Sustainable Systems. http://css.snre.umich.edu/css_doc/CSS09–05.pdf. Accessed December 27, 2012.

Chapple, Candace. "Northern Michigan Loves Stand-Up Paddle Boarding." MyNorth.com. http://www.mynorth.com/My-North/June-2012/Northern-Michigan-Stand-Up-Paddle-Boarding-The-Latest-Great-Lakes-Fad/. Accessed December 28, 2012.

Ellis, Alvina Wagner. *My Life on the Beautiful Betsie River.* Elk Rapids, MI: Bookability, 2006.

"Explore Michigan's Other Half." Wet Mitten Surf Shop. http://www.wet mittensurfshop.com/Michigan-Surfing-Information-s/1854.htm. Accessed December 29, 2012.

Klug, Fritz. "Kalamazoo River Oil Spill: Environmental Group Calls for More Pipeline Safety Standards, Accountability." Mlive.com, July 23, 2012. http://www.mlive.com/news/kalamazoo/index.ssf/2012/07/kalamazoo_river_oil_spill_envi.html. Accessed November 7, 2012.

Michigan Heritage Water Trails. http://www.wmich.edu/glcms/watertrails/. Accessed November 5, 2012.

Chapter 4

"Grand Hotel Recognized for 'Green Initiatives.'" Berg Muirhead and Associates, April 10, 2009. http://www.grandhotel.com/pdfs/grand-hotel-green-initiatives.pdf. Accessed October 12, 2012.

"How Many Islands Are in the Great Lakes?" The Nature Conservancy, August 20, 2010. http://www.mnn.com/local-reports/michigan/nature-conservancy/how-many-islands-are-in-the-great-lakes. Accessed October 12, 2012.

"Lime Island Designated Newest State Recreation Area." Michigan Department of Natural Resources, June 29, 2011. http://www.michigan.gov/dnr/0,4570,7–153–10371_10402–258538—,00.html. Accessed October 12, 2012.

"Lime Island Master Plan." Michigan Department of Natural Resources, September 15, 2004. http://www.michigan.gov/documents/Lime IslandMasterPlanFinalDraft9–15–04_164726_7.pdf. Accessed October 12, 2012.

"Munising Ice Formations." Great Lakes Waterfalls & Beyond. Last updated March 25, 2008. http://www.gowaterfalling.com/waterfalls/places/munis ingice.shtml. Accessed December 30, 2012.

Sleeping Bear Dunes National Lakeshore. National Park Service. http://www .nps.gov/slbe/index.htm. Accessed October 12, 2012.

Chapter 5

"EHD—Outbreak of Epizootic Hemorrhagic Disease in Deer." Emerging Disease Issues, Michigan.gov. http://www.michigan.gov/emergingdiseases /0,4579,7-186—283966—,00.html. Accessed December 4, 2012.

"Fun with Bat Houses and Wood Duck Nesting Boxes." General Motors/Chevrolet. May 14, 2012. http://media.gm.com/media/us/en/chevrolet/news .detail.html/content/Pages/news/us/en/2012/May/05014_bathouse.html. Accessed December 4, 2012.

Hartig, John. "Extreme Makeover at Detroit River Refuge." U.S. Fish and Wildlife Service/National Wildlife Refuge System. Last updated November 5, 2012. http://www.fws.gov/refuges/RefugeUpdate/NovDec_2012/extreme makeover.html. Accessed December 4, 2012.

"Hibernating Bats at Tippy Hydro Highest Number to Date." Consumers Energy, March 28, 2012. http://consumersenergyinyourcommunity.wordpress .com/2012/03/28/hibernating-bats-at-tippy-hydro-at-highest-number-to-date/. Accessed December 4, 2012.

Kantner, Shannon. "DNR Changes Deer Hunting Rules." WILX.com, November 13, 2012. http://www.wilx.com/news/headlines/DNR-Limits-Firearm-Licenses-Due-to-Deer-Disease—179049551.html. Accessed December 27, 2012.

"Michigan Elk: Past and Present." Michigan Department of Natural Resources. http://www.michigan.gov/dnr/0,4570,7-153-10363_10856_10893-28275—,00.html. Accessed December 4, 2012.

"Michigan Wildlife Viewing Guide." Michigan Department of Natural Resources. http://www.michigandnr.com/publications/pdfs/wildlife/viewing guide/default.htm. Accessed December 4, 2012.

"Michigan Wolf Management Plan." Michigan Department of Natural Resources, July 10, 2008. http://www.michigan.gov/documents/dnr/Draft_Wolf_Management_Plan_030708_227742_7.pdf. Accessed December 4, 2012.

"Monarch Butterfly Migration." Bays de Noc Convention & Visitors Bureau. http://www.travelbaysdenoc.com/?MonarchButterflyMigration. Accessed December 4, 2012.

"Natural Resources Commission Authorized Limited Public Wolf Harvest Aimed at Managing Wolf Population." Michigan Department of Natural Resources. http://www.michigan.gov/dnr/0,4570,7-153-10371_10402-308071--,00.html. Accessed July 29, 2013.

"Urban Wildlife Viewing." Michigan Department of Natural Resources. http://www.michigan.gov/dnr/0,4570,7-153-10370_12144-35569—,00.html. Accessed December 4, 2012.

Chapter 6

Beecham, Tara. "How Green is Your Tee?" *Stormwater,* March 16, 2000. http://www.stormh20.com/SW/Articles/How_Green_Is_Your_Tee_16519.aspx. Accessed October 21, 2012.

Keagle, Lauri Harvey. "Greener Greens: How Benton Harbor went from a Giant Brownfield to Lustrous, Lakefront Nicklaus." *Harbor Shores News,* May 26, 2010. http://www.ehow.com/how_5836231_send-song-cell-phone.html. Accessed October 21, 2012.

"Matters of Scale—Planet Golf." *World Watch Magazine,* April 2004. http://www.worldwatch.org/node/797 (Accessed December 27, 2012).

Olmsted, Larry. "Golf Loving Michigan Welcomes Visitors—And Second Major of the Season." *Forbes,* July, 5, 2012. http://www.forbes.com/sites/larryolmsted/2012/07/05/golf-loving-michigan-welcomes-visitors-and-second-major-of-the-season/. Accessed October 20, 2012.

Wexler, Mark. "Green Golf is Growing—Slowly." National Geographic News. June 25, 2004. http://go.microsoft.com/fwlink/?LinkId=30857&clcid=0x409 (Accessed October 20, 2012).

"Who is the Grand Traverse Band?" Gtband.org, March 2011. http://www.gtbindians.org/images/pdf_files/march_web_sect3.pdf. Accessed October 12, 2012.

Chapter 7

"Climate Change." National Park Service/Pictured Rocks National Lakeshore. 2009. http://www.nps.gov/piro/naturescience/climate-change.htm. Accessed October 8, 2012.

"Green Initiatives." Michigan Department of Natural Resources. http://www.michigan.gov/dnr/0,4570,7-153-10773-24871—,00.html. Accessed October 1, 2012.

"Green Parks Plan." National Park Service/U.S. Department of the Interior,

April 2012. http://www.nps.gov/greenparksplan/downloads/NPS_2012_ Green_Parks_Plan.pdf. Accessed November 15, 2012.

"The Headlands—An Emmet County Park on the Straits of Mackinac." Emmet County, Michigan. http://www.emmetcounty.org/headlands/. Accessed November 18, 2012.

Chapter 8

CityFlatsHotel. http://www.cityflatshotel.com/. Accessed December 2, 2012.

"Green Lodging Michigan—Recognizing Michigan's Hospitality Industry." Michigan.gov. http://www.michigan.gov/mdcd/0,1607,7-122-25676_25677 _37026—-,00.html. Accessed October 4, 2012.

"Hotels and Motels." Energy Star. U.S. Environmental Agency. Last updated December 2007. http://www.energystar.gov/index.cfm?c=business.EPA_ BUM_CH12_HotelsMotels#S_12_1 _http://www.starwoodpromos.com/ westingreenchoice/more/Hotel.pdf?1184-46b5. Accessed December 1, 2012.

"Make a Green Choice." Westin Hotels & Resorts. http://www.microsoft.com/ isapi/redir.dll?prd=ie&ar=windowsmedia. Accessed December 3, 2012.

Chapter 9

"Bishop Baraga—Shrine of the Snowshoe Priest." Roadsideamerica.com. http:// www.roadsideamerica.com/story/11140. Accessed December 8, 2012.

"Celebrating Wildflowers." U.S. Forest Service. http://www.fs.fed.us/wildflow ers/regions/eastern/LodaLake/index.shtml. Accessed December 29, 2012.

"Explore the Trap Hills on the North Country Trail!" North Country Trail Association. Last updated November 18, 2012. http://www.northcountrytrail .org/pwf/traphills.htm#Why%20the%20Trap%20Hhttp://www.summit post.org/greenstone-ridge-isle-royale/191040ills. Accessed December 15, 2012.

Hansen, Eric. "Out of Sight: Hiking Michigan's Trap Hills." *Backpacker,* May 2002. http://www.backpacker.com/may_2002_destinations_michigan_ trap_hills/destinations/4749. Accessed December 1, 2012.

Hollowell, Dana. "Cycling Tourists, Rails-to-Trails Boost Michigan as a Two-Wheeled Vacation Destination." MLive Michigan, April 5, 2012. http:// www.mlive.com/business/index.ssf/2012/04/cycling_tourists_rails-to-trai. html. Accessed December 6, 2012.

Hubbell, Amy. "Dunes' Attendance Keeps Soaring." *Leelanau Enterprise,* August 9, 2012. http://www.leelanaunews.com/news/2012–08–09/Front_Page/Dunes_attendance_keeps_soaring.html. Accessed December 1, 2012.

"The Leave No Trace Seven Principles." Leave No Trace Center for Outdoor Ethics. http://lnt.org/learn/7-principlessleeping%20bear%20lakeshore%20visitors%202012. Accessed December 4, 2012.

"Thunder Bay Karst Preserve." The Michigan Karst Conservancy. http://www.caves.org/conservancy/mkc/preserve_tb.html. Accessed December 31, 2012.

Epilogue

Heimbuch, Jaymi. "6 Green Must-Haves for Winter." Planetgreen.com, December 10, 2008. http://planetgreen.discovery.com/travel-outdoors/winter-outdoor-gear.html. Accessed December 26, 2012.

Louv, Richard. *Last Child in the Woods.* Chapel Hill, NC: Algonquin Books, 2008.

INDEX